PUBLIC POLICY
IN A NEW KEY

Other Books by Amitai Etzioni

The Spirit of Community:
Rights, Responsibilities and the Communication Agenda (1993)

A Responsive Society (1991)

The Moral Dimension:
Toward a New Economics (1988)

Capital Corruption:
The New Attack on American Democracy (1984)

An Immodest Agenda:
Rebuilding America Before the Twenty-First Century (1983)

Genetic Fix:
The Next Technological Revolution (1973)

The Active Society:
A Theory of Societal and Political Processes (1968)

Political Unification:
A Comparative Study of Leaders and Forces (1965)

Modern Organizations (1964)

A Comparative Analysis of Complex Organizations (1961)

PUBLIC POLICY
IN A NEW KEY

Amitai Etzioni

Transaction Publishers
New Brunswick (U.S.A.) and London (U.K.)

Library of Congress Catalog Number: 92-20089
ISBN: 1-56000-075-9
Printed in the United States of America

Library of Congress Cataloging-in-Publication Data
Etzioni, Amitai.
  Public policy in a new key / Amitai Etzioni.
    p.   cm.
  ISBN 1-56000-075-9 (cloth)
  1. Policy sciences.   2. Competition.   3. Post-communism.   I. Title.
H97.E84   1992
361.6'1—dc20

                                                                    92-20089
                                                                    CIP

For my colleagues who care

Contents

Acknowledgments

I gratefully acknowledge the research assistance provided by Barry Kreiswirth, Lauren Levy, and Sharon Pressner in the preparation of this book. My thanks also go to Barbara Hoch Marcus who acted as editorial coordinator for this project.

For the discussion of rights proliferation in chapter 3, I am indebted to the executive director of the American Alliance for Rights and Responsibilities, Roger Conner, to Gerda Bikales of AACR for numerous comments and suggestions, and to Judith Lurie and Darin Levine for research assistance.

On health-maintenance issues discussed in chapter 5, extensive research assistance was provided by Heather Karp, and comments by Allan Brandt, Paul Cleary, and Mary Jo Good proved very helpful.

Finally, I am grateful to Darin Levine for his research assistance on the policy implications of socio-economics presented in chapter 7.

Preface

What is the underlying framework of the policy analysis that is practiced in these pages? First of all, it is sociology broadly conceived. The conceptual and theoretical tools that have been brought to bear are those of a person who has spent a lifetime studying sociology—although I have drawn liberally from sister social sciences such as political science and psychology and, above all, from what I call socio-economics (itself a mixture of economics and other social sciences). A person using only the conceptual apparatus of, say, legal analysis or neoclassical economics would be likely to focus on different factors and might well come to different conclusions.

I freely admit that I do not consider all the tools of analysis to be equally powerful. But I also believe that more is at work than that I was trained as a sociologist, and hence I am partial to its powers. The underlying reason that sociology broadly conceived is powerful is that what we are dealing with are societal problems. If the questions at hand were what laws are applicable to an issue or what the price of tomatoes would be next season, the same tools would not do as well. As Veblen long ago noted, the more deeply one is involved in one discipline, the more one acquires what he called a "trained incapacity" in others.

The difference in perspective is especially highlighted in the first essay of this volume, the subject of which is the societal transformation of post-Communist societies. My colleagues who are neoclassical economists have been dishing out advice to Poland and, more recently, to the former USSR about how to rush into creating democratic and capitalist regimes. But there is precious little in neoclassical theory that deals with societal changes (or, for that matter, with macroeconomic changes, the theory basically being one of comparative statistics). No wonder their policy analysis has reached rather different conclusions than those a sociologist would reach. I leave it to the reader to determine which works to better effect.

Perhaps the term *sociology* never was, and certainly no longer is, a sufficient description of the discipline. There are fundamentally different kinds of sociology. The one that I have utilized in these essays may be called "macrosociology," because it deals with societies, their constituting units and combinations, rather than with interpersonal relations, small groups, and such. Although I hope these essays may enrich the discipline of sociology, their primary purpose is to apply the tools of sociology to address the major issues that society faces these days, such as competitiveness, the rise in health-care costs, and massive political corruption.

Last, but not least, the analysis is critical and draws upon values. It is critical in the sense that it seeks to support change. As a rule, a person who is satisfied with the way things are seeks no change and requires no policy analysis. "Steady as she goes" typically entails holding on to the wheel, maybe performing some routine maintenance, but no systematic working out of new structures and processes, new departures, that is policy analysis.

Values enter of necessity, because to favor change means choosing the alternative future toward which one aspires to advance. Take the discussion of political corruption. It clearly indicates a commitment to the notion of one person, one vote. Those who accept the notion that those who are richer—and hence are more successful in terms of our market economy and better at manipulating the political system—are entitled to an extra say in Washington and the state capitals, will find very little to support in the analysis provided below. Similarly, while my analysis of the demerits of the suggested policies of health-care rationing is in part based on the illogic of many of the suggestions, I also draw on a moral commitment that we should not terminate the lives of people who are conscious. Those who believe that once we reach a certain age (eighty-two has been suggested, to be ratcheted down in bad economic times) we have exhausted our claim on the assets of the society and should be given only ameliorative, and not therapeutic, care will not find the following analysis morally acceptable.

Some members of the press have wondered how one may treat subjects as widely diverse as health care, competitiveness, and political corruption, among others. Some have even called me an "everything expert," which is not a compliment, especially in academic circles. The "secret" is actually quite simple and open: the kind of social science analysis that is applied here is like a universal key that opens many doors. I am not an expert on health care, competitiveness, or political systems. However, when these and numerous other topics are examined from the viewpoint advanced here, one gains insights and establishes findings that would otherwise not be readily visible. I make no claim to exhaust these subjects, the way a specialist might. I do suggest, however, that such analysis allows us to get a handle on them that would otherwise not be possible.

Readers who find this kind of policy analysis of interest may wish to join a growing group of colleagues that meets annually under the auspices of the Society for the Advancement of Socio-Economics, to exchange ideas and to further extend the approach. If I am sure of anything, it is that such policy analysis, in the key in which it is played here, requires much more elaboration and extension.

1

Jump versus Gradual Transition to Capitalism in Poland and Russia

Two Views of Friction

During the deliberations of a faculty seminar on socio-economics at The George Washington University in 1986-7, before the dramatic developments in Eastern Europe, the question of the pace of socio-economic change kept coming up. For a while it seemed that regardless of the topic to which a particular session of the seminar was devoted, the main difference in perspective between those seminar members who were neoclassical economists and the other social scientists present was their divergent assumptions about the pace of human adjustments to new situations and signals. The neoclassical economists tended to assume that the adjustments would be swift and basically unproblematic. That is, while forgoing the assumption that economics formerly embraced, of instantaneous and cost-free adjustments, the neoclassicists continued to hold that the hindering factors, or friction, were so low that they did not require significant modifications to the assumptions and basic model, or

This chapter was first drafted as an article shortly after the collapse of communism in Poland in 1989. At that time, those who urged a "jump to capitalism" suggested that it would take two years to accomplish the transition. Earlier and shorter versions of the article published at that time predicted that either the transition would be slowed down or democracy would not be able to persevere.[1] The jury is still out as to whose counsel—jump or go gradually—was the correct one. Evidence presented in the current version, however, shows that a jump was not possible, and that the attempts to rush the transition caused strains that are endangering the budding democracy in Poland. While this is not discussed here, note that countries that moved more gradually, especially Hungary, are doing better economically and politically than Poland. Most important, as these lines are written early in 1992, Russia just launched a jump into capitalism. Our prediction is now applied to that country as well: Slow down or you will end up breaking the neck of the nascent democracy.

1

to the lists of factors that need to be systematically studied, or to the predictions of neoclassical economics. The possibility of slow and costly adjustments to changes—or high friction—was acknowledged. It was treated, however, as if it did not occur or was rare. Thus, while no one in the seminar denied that behavior was "sticky," when the discussion turned to specifics (for instance, to the effects of price increases on energy conservation), neoclassical economists tended to suggest that conservation would follow once prices were increased. Similarly, it was recognized that prices are sticky on the downside, but that recognition did not leave any discernible imprints on the neoclassicists' discussion about the use of short-term recessions as a way to curb inflation, and so on.

In contrast, other social scientists in the seminar tended to point to a long list of observations that people "just did not behave that way," that they were much slower to adjust than the neoclassical economists expected. Examples abound: many Americans were slow to open IRA accounts although it was clearly to their advantage to do so; they were slow to leave jobs in declining industries and move from depressed parts of the country to new and rising ones; they continued to buy about the same number of tax shelters even after the 1986 tax law made them much less favorable; they kept inefficient corporations going right next to more efficient ones. While these members of the seminar initially expressed the thesis in absolute terms, that is, behavior does not conform to neoclassical expectations, they gradually came to express the thesis in relative terms. Rather than assuming that people do not change, the preferred formula became that changes in personal and social behavior, including economic, tend to be slow and difficult, that friction is high.

Once both groups of seminar members became aware that they were focusing on the same kind of factor, friction, the door opened to questions regarding the typical extent of friction, the factors that account for the particular level found, and the implications of high levels of friction for various models and predictions. The seminar stopped, more or less, at this point. This article provides a preliminary discussion of these questions.

Another way to highlight the issue at hand is to return to an often-repeated analogue that neoclassical economists use when challenged that their theories are "unrealistic." They respond that their models are like those of physicists: they formulate laws for perfect conditions, for example, a frictionless slope. These laws provide either an approximation or a model that can then be adjusted to the empirical situation. Socio-economists may respond (at least this one does) that a model may serve as a suitable approximation when it actually does approximate, that is, comes reasonably close to the reality it seeks to model. However, just as the assumption of imperfect information implies that information is almost fully available (while in actuality decisions are made with only small fractions of the needed information), so the model of a frictionless slope is productive only to the extent that the relevant segments of the world under study are rather low in friction. If friction, like ignorance (in effect a form of friction), is typically high, the suggested logic of model building favors the use of a model of complete friction and adjustments that reflect whatever movement one does encounter.

In the area of decision making, this suggests, first, that one should assume that poor decisions, made with little information and poor processing of the information that is available, are the norm. Well-informed, "good" (not to mention optimal) decisions are the exceptions, and the special factors that account for them need explaining. This is, of course, the opposite of the tack usually taken, in which one tries to account for irrationality, assuming rationality to be normal.[2] Second, unlike physicists, neoclassical economists do not provide, in most areas, transition coefficients, that is, formulas that allow one to move from generalizations about the idealized state, the frictionless slope, to movement on actual slopes. This omission is unimportant if friction is very low, but critical if it is high. As we shall see immediately, at least in some rather important cases, friction is high indeed; hence, the need for a new approach.

Friction and Post-Communist Transitions

The extent of friction, the ease and the speed with which socio-economic changes can be introduced, is pivotal to the evaluation of the policies pursued and urged on various post-Communist countries since 1989. At the same time, the lessons of these transitions help evolve theories about the levels of friction and the determining factors—theorems that, we shall see, apply to many other areas of socio-economic change, from industrial development to movement toward freer trade.

Up to 1992, Poland was the only post-Communist country that had followed neoclassicists' advice to jump from a command-and-control system into a free market, or "shock therapy," as others have put it. Shock therapy began January 1, 1990. The most outspoken American proponent of such shock therapy is Jeffrey Sachs, a Harvard economist retained by Solidarity and the governments of Russia and other Eastern European nations. Sachs's argument is neatly encapsulated by the remark of an Eastern European economist he quotes approvingly: "You don't try to cross over a chasm in two leaps." Sachs also stated, in an interview with the *Christian Science Monitor*, "It is repeatedly shown throughout history that gradualism in such a deep crisis doesn't work. . . so if you don't act decisively, it constantly gets ahead of you."[3] He explained earlier:

> My idea is to create the market system as quickly as possible. Let people start to operate. The other idea is to say "Well, we understand that we're punishing the private sector brutally, that none of this makes any sense, but let's only change things very gradually so that maybe in ten years we'll have a normal business environment." That's a crazy idea, frankly.[4]

"The economic textbooks say such a program is to be preferred to a step-by-step program," Heinrich Machewskin, an economist with the German Institute for the Economy in Berlin, stated.[5] Gary Becker of the University of Chicago wrote that "land, housing, retail establishments, and many services can become private property right away. . . . It would even be technically possible to privatize many large factories quickly." Becker added, "The duration of the pain can be reduced and benefits increased if the essentials of a market system are quickly put into place."[6]

In January 1992 Russia became the second former Communist society to attempt "shock therapy," following the advice of Western economists and pressure from the United States and the International Monetary Fund (IMF). Leading economists advised Russia and the other former Soviet republics to move even more swiftly than Eastern Europe to tackle economic changes.[7] Jeffrey Sachs, who is also advising Russia, acknowledged that it will be more difficult for the Soviet Union to jump to capitalism, but added that the fact that "it is a harder case doesn't change the policy design."[8]

I predicted that the transition in Poland would either be slowed down or repudiated.[9] The prediction was based on observing specific socioeconomic factors (to be discussed shortly) that suggested that the friction level of transition would be high, and therefore that attempts to move rapidly would generate stress that could not be overcome, at least within a democratic framework. The first sign that this seemed to be a valid prediction could be seen in the results of the November 1990 elections.

A *Washington Post* headline read: "Mazowiecki Steps Down as Premier: Government Policies Seen as Repudiated by Polish Electorate." Lech Walesa won with 40 percent of the votes; Stanislaw Tyminski, an obscure émigré businessman, won 23 percent; and Mazowiecki received only 18 percent of the votes.[10]

Neoclassical economists tend to assume that people are the same in all societies, cultures, and historical situations: they are rationally seeking to maximize their self-interest. According to neoclassicists, in Communist societies people are only held back by overbearing statist institutions, and scrapping those will free their entrepreneurial spirit and lead in short order to a free economy. Building on these assumptions, urged upon them by neoclassical economists and backed up by pressure from international institutions (such as the IMF and the World Bank), as well as the U.S. State Department and some American banks and private investors, in 1990 Poland slashed government subsidies, made the *zloty* convertible, closed or privatized a number of state enterprises, deregulated, and allowed freedom of labor mobility, and otherwise made room for the market-based allocation of resources. It was assumed that as resources were "privatized," or freed from state control, the market would deliver them where they would be used most effectively.

For a short transition period, measured in a year or two, high inflation and unemployment were expected; but thereafter, the economy was expected to adjust without any particular state interventions to guide the new resources to this or that place, and without any social safeguards. In Poland, just prior to implementation of the new program, "government officials predict[ed] that after a turbulent six months or so the economy should begin to stabilize."[11] "Sure, there will be momentary dislocations; prices will undergo a sharp initial rise. But then they'll stabilize. People will know where they stand."[12] The same held for the eastern parts of Germany, where rapid transition has also been attempted. In mid-1990, "the German Economic Research Institute predict[ed] stabilization [for eastern Germany] late next year and a turnaround in 1992."[13] Eight months later, with the bill for economic recovery still rising, "estimates on the cost of rebuilding eastern Germany have been steadily raised as the region's economic woes multiplied. Many economists now predict that it will cost Bonn more than $1 trillion over the next decade. This year, economists estimate, the Government will have to provide close to $100 billion. . ." "Many economists still predict that an upswing will begin next year [for eastern Germany] that could eventually rival the 'economic miracle' of West Germany's postwar reconstruction. . . ,"[14] a prediction that was clearly not in line with the events that followed. More and more observers admitted that, in terms of the former Soviet Union, "conversion. . . to an effective market-based system is likely to take 10 or 15 years, at least."[15] There is little evidence to support these optimistic predictions.

The rise of street vendors in Poland was hailed as a sign that the transition was taking place as expected. It was seen also as evidence that Poland was full of entrepreneurs and managers who could run private businesses given a free market.

> Tens of thousands of Poles have turned streets, open spaces, even whole sports stadiums into vast bazaars, selling everything imaginable at rock-bottom prices: from shoelaces to fur coats, plastic flowers to ghetto blasters, denim jackets to skateboards.[16]

> The new free-market forces were at work. . . on the sidewalk in front of an official state grocery store. . where on Thursday afternoon hundreds of shoppers were crowding about to buy fresh meat, sausage, butter, sugar and coffee. In the not too distant past, inquiries for these goods in stores notable for their bare shelves would bring the response "nie ma," or "we don't have any." The merchandise was being sold on Thursday from more than 20 trucks, private cars and even upturned cartons on the sidewalk clustered about an old sign in front of the government store proclaiming, "It is forbidden to sell around this building.". . . *What is going on here is precisely the kind of capitalist initiative and competition that Finance Minister Leszek Balcerowicz and other officials hope will bring prices down and renew the economy.* (Emphasis added)[17]

What are the socio-economic factors that suggest that Poland will be forced to slow down its economic transition or abort its democratic government, and to what extent can they be generalized to other situations?

Human Factors

Far from having fixed, self-interested preferences, individuals are penetrated by the institutions and cultures in which they spend their formative years and various parts of their adulthood. True, underneath their acculturation there are elementary basic human features. However, these are not the quest for profit, but the quest for affection, self-esteem, and self-expression, aside from the need for basic creature comforts. In addition, these needs can be significantly perverted by the particular societal structures in which people are formed and in which they function.

Many (albeit not all) Poles, citizens of other post-Communist societies, and citizens of many less developed countries have acquired specific personality traits and work habits that cannot be modified on short order. These include working slowly and without undue exertion, not taking initiatives or responsibilities, stressing quantity over quality, featherbedding, using work time for other purposes (especially shopping), expecting promotions based on irrelevant considerations such as party loyalties and connections, barter of work time and material for other favors, and low-technology approaches.

The transition to the Western style of work and competition will meet resistance. In Yugoslavia, 40 percent of the workers at McDonald's quit because the work was too strenuous.[18] Others, especially older workers in manual labor such as shipyards and steel mills, are hard to retrain for work in new, high-tech industries, say, computer programming. All this holds, only more so, for the many who have served a lifetime as bureaucrats, party commissars, and teachers of Marxism and Leninism—and those who have spent their lives verifying that others are toeing the line.

Shock therapy also ignores the basic concept of division of labor, explains Valtr Komarek, the former Czechoslovak deputy prime minister and director of the Forecasting Institute of the Academy of Sciences in Prague: "Most of the people of Czechoslovakia, Poland, and Russia," he says, "have committed their lives to developing highly specialized skills for heavy industries. Vast numbers of people are being asked to abandon their training and experience, and, without an adequate adjustment phase, take part in an amorphous 'market' building itself up from scratch." Eastern Europeans, he says, should concentrate on their major industries to compete in the world economy, and that the government should protect these industries and "make sure their citizens are not cast adrift."[19]

Management and entrepreneurial skills are in particularly short supply. The skills and personality attributes of street vendors, as indirectly pointed out by Max Weber in his discussion of the difference between mercantilism and capitalism, are not those needed. The typical orientation of these street "capitalists" is toward quick bucks, which they achieve with short-term responses to immediate demands and next to no investment (and hence no capital management) or management of a significant labor force—not to mention long-run planning, innovation, or research and development. They are after quick profits, not reinvesting back into enterprises to build major businesses. This observation is supported by the fact that despite the explosive growth of small traders in Poland, the country is very short of managers for sizable enterprises. In Poland, "it is no small feat to find people who are both experienced managers and untarnished by links to the discredited old system. There is a prejudice against filling posts with people who managed state-run enterprises under Communist rule. But often they are the most qualified, or the only qualified, people available."[20]

Many of those who function successfully are repatriated Polish Americans, who are far too few to make a difference to the economy as a whole. The Polish-American Enterprise Fund is reliably reported to have been unable to find qualified takers for most of its funds, reflecting the shortage of true managers and entrepreneurs.[21] Typically, loans are below the $50,000 level. (In Third World countries in similar stages of development, it is common to refer to this problem as a lack of, or low, absorptive capacity.) All this is not to suggest that the needed capitalistic skills and traits cannot be developed in Poland, that its people are somehow inherently inferior; only that their development requires years, if not decades (as it took in the United States under much more favorable circumstances). Introducing large-scale capital, at this stage in the form of foreign aid, is often largely wasted.[22]

Capitalism has also brought with it increased scandal and scams. The Poles have been quick learners in this area—everything from check kiting to illegal imports—which has cost the government millions of dollars.[23] Corruption has not been limited to petty thieves, but has reached high echelons. Grzegorz Wojtowicz, the chairman of Poland's central bank, was pulled off a train and thrown into jail for allowing a check kiter to cost the state $360 million. Janusz Sawicki, the country's chief debt negotiator, was fired for losing track of between $150 million and $863 million.[24] In Russia, in the winter of 1992, relief from the West was severely hampered because most of the food and medical supplies that arrived in airports and harbors was stolen.

Lena Kolarska Bobinska, a Polish sociologist, stated:

> There has been a lot of discussion about whether to transform the country rapidly or slowly, as though we were referring to an athletic contest. Few people have anything to say about where we are hurrying to; what kind of capitalism is going to emerge;

how much the state should intervene and how much should be left to unfettered market forces; whether we want a welfare state which will subsidize housing, education, health care, and so on, but levy higher taxes, or whether we want lower taxes and a system closer to that preferred by the liberals in which everyone has to look out for him- or herself. . . . It's high time we thought about the long term and stopped assessing change simply in terms of how we managed to distance ourselves from Communism.[25]

Capital

Neoclassical economists tend to assume that if state enterprises are closed or "privatized" (by which they mean legal title is changed from the state to stockholders), the capital assets that are released will float on their own to where the highest "price" or return is available for them in the free market. Capital will thus be much more efficiently used, and productivity will rise. (They correctly point to "horror stories" that are the result of capital being allocated not to users, who are the most willing to pay for it, but distributed by government, based on national or social ambitions, leading to the grossly excessive production of expensive and other goods.)

Recent experience, however, raises serious doubts about the assumption of the ready transfer of capital by private corporations, which are either using previously state-owned assets or selling them and using the yield for new investments. As an American economist who works in Poland put it (an observation that is also confirmed in eastern Germany and other post-Communist countries): "When you open them to the free market, Communists' capital assets dissolve like an Alka-Seltzer pill in a glass of water."[26] Large amounts of the assets used in Communist economies are neither transferable nor salable. Barbara Piasecka Johnson's much-publicized plan to buy a controlling share of the Gdansk Shipyard "ran into many of the obstacles that have tripped up other Westerners seeking to invest in Eastern Europe: difficulties in assessing the value of enterprises, daunting investments needed for modernization. . . . "[27] The following year this item appeared: "Interflug, the East German state airline, once touted as one of the country's jewels, will be shut down. The Treuhand [the holding company created by the government to privatize 8,000 enterprises controlled by the former East German state] could not find a buyer."[28] *The Wall Street Journal* reports that potential investors are reluctant due to "the lack of infrastructure such as telecommunications and transportation, a weak network of suppliers, and East

German companies' debt."[29] Hence, often the short-run effect of privatization is not a rise in output, but a sharp decline in the GNP, mass unemployment, and recession. In Poland "the economy also fell into a deep recession, with industrial output falling 30 percent. Farm production slowed and real pay declined by 40 percent, according to estimates."[30] A year after the new economic program was implemented in Poland, "unemployment has climbed to one million, and next year could reach two million, or more than 11 percent." [31] Joseph Berliner, a research fellow at Harvard's Russian Research Center, says that the "capital stock buildup [in Russia] under decades of nonmarket planning is grossly out of sync with the structure of capital that the market would call for."[32]

Like other developing nations, post-Communist societies will have to raise new capital mainly from gradually saving, a very painful and slow process in face of a sharply declining standard of living. A major socio-economic point needs to be mentioned here. Two facts combine to make such saving particularly difficult in post-Communist societies: first, the standard of living is in part a subjective matter, and second, losses raise much more resistance than foregone gains of similar magnitude.[33] Hence, while a country that had always had a very low standard of living might be able to save when its standard of living rises above the subsistence level, this is more difficult for a country like Poland which had a higher standard of living but is losing part of it due to transition. Theoretically, other countries could provide a steady flow of capital as the capacity to absorb is gradually increased, but the amounts involved and the long-run commitment needed are such that this is unlikely to obviate the need for slow self-generation of capital. In fact, according to Jeffrey Sachs, Russia needs international support of approximately 5 percent of its $300 billion GNP—around $15 billion a year—for the next four or five years.[34] To raise the East to the West's industrial level, Sachs, writing in The *Economist*, proposes that about $30 billion a year go to Russia and the other republics for the next three to four years.[35]

It should be noted that even under the much more favorable conditions in the contemporary United States, closed steel mills are not readily converted into high-tech industries. The fallacy of the notion that capital is readily convertible and that it can be accomplished without substantial losses—a reflection of what might be called capital friction—was clearly seen when attempts were made to convert corporations that specialize in military production to other uses. Murray Weidenbaum, former chair of the President's Council of Economic Advisors, states: "Every comprehensive study of past attempts by large defense contractors to use their capabilities beyond the aerospace market has failed to find a single important example of success."[36]

Infrastructure

Generally, for an economy to take off into higher reaches of development, certain elements must be in place. I have spelled out elsewhere the reasons for the particular list that follows:[37] reliable flows of inanimate energy; means of low-cost, expeditious and reliable transportation; communications; and supportive financial and legal institutions. Post-Communist countries, like many less developed countries, are short on all of these. Poland, for example, is suffering from its dependence on oil from Russia and needs time to adjust to the reduction of oil from this source or its rapid increase in price. Poland's telecommunications are woefully unadapted: it has seven phone lines for every 100 people.[38] Its banking system is primitive: transactions are done in cash; there is no tradition of check writing or bank credits, not to mention stock markets, private savings, and investments.

> At the PKO bank in Warsaw, [Andrzej] Makacewicz [president of the Polish Foundation, a private organization set up to assist economic change]. . . had been standing in line for an hour, trying to deposit 100 million zlotys—about $10,500—that he had hand-carried from a PKO branch bank in Gdansk, a four-hour drive away, because interbank transfers can take months.[39]

Transportation facilities are inadequate for a modern economy. In eastern Germany, "the region's roads, railways, airports, and telecommunications are so rundown that a recent report by western Germany's Kiel Institute described them as 'wholly inadequate for the rapid development of the five new federal states.'"[40]

One of the reasons Western capital has been so reluctant to rush in is the confusion of laws and the dangers of political instability. It will take time to demonstrate to the West a reasonable measure of political continuity. Foreign investors realize that just as it is easy to slash confiscatory and restrictive laws, they can be quickly reinstated, unless they are supported by considerable tradition, political culture, and public support. (The rapid way China flip-flops on its "democratization" is a case in point.)

Labor Mobility

Closing down industries (shipyards, steel mills) that the state maintained for noneconomic reasons and developing new ones that are more responsive to the market often entail labor mobility. In the United States, if the car industry (sustained in part by state supports in the form of bailouts and limitations on imported cars) is in decline and oil on the rise, labor moves from Michigan to Texas. Such movement assumes, first of all, a tradition of mobility that is strong in the United States but much weaker in other countries. People in Poland are much less accustomed to leaving behind their extended families, communities, and graves. Additionally, political conditions often prevented a tradition of free mobility to grow. (The fact that some people do emigrate does not show that the rest are equally mobile; on the contrary, those less adaptable are those who are predisposed to stay.)

Last but not least, there is an interactive effect between labor mobility and the shortage of capital. Since houses, schools, hospitals, and shops obviously cannot move with labor, the greater the capital shortage, all other things being equal, the more difficult it is for labor to move and the slower the transition from one industry to another.

Values

Neoclassical economists assume that once people overthrow the tyranny of Communist political institutions, they exhibit the basic human proclivity to pursue self-interest and self-satisfaction. It is true that some Communist followers made a surprisingly rapid transition to Western values (or at least slogans), and for some, privatization has acquired the same standing of a simple cure-all that nationalization once had. But most members of these societies have kept a variety of social values, not easily compatible with capitalism, especially the raw kind urged on Poland. Mieczyslaw Kabal, an economist with the Labor Research Institute in Warsaw, stated: "In the Eastern European value system, the right to work and job security are very important values."[41] "There have been reports [in Hungary] of enterprise managers cutting sweetheart deals with Western investors offering to take their firms private for artificially low prices in return for guaranteed jobs and pay."[42] In Poland the minister of privatization, Waldemar Kuczynski, "is also frustrated that many managers of newly privatized companies have sharply raised prices to increase profits, rather than improve production and service."[43]

In Czechoslovakia there is considerable opposition to a policy that seeks to convert arms plants, since arms manufacture is the country's largest industry and employer. Arms have been sold to Syria, to the displeasure of the West, in order to receive hard currency. Jozef Blahusiak, of the Slovak Economics Ministry, observed that the trade unions fight any move that will result in job losses, but without the Soviet Union it is difficult to find buyers for the peaceful products he hopes will replace arms.[44]

The evidence shows, especially from China and the USSR in its last year, that successful farmers and "cooperatives" (private enterprises) do not evoke in others the American desire to keep up with the Joneses and thus multiply the capitalist spirit at "making it." Instead, these ventures frequently bring forth a strong yearning for egalitarianism, combined with pressure to tax heavily those who are successful. Charles P. Wallace reports: "The relatively large sums being earned by cooperatives [in the USSR] have aroused a considerable amount of jealousy, both from state institutions that work far less efficiently and private workers who grumble about the disparity in their take-home pay."[45] These are hardly the sentiments that foster entrepreneurial capitalism.

In Poland ownership of houses and apartments, land, and factories is being returned to those who had title before the Communist takeover, allowing fairness and justice to take precedence over economic efficiency. (In Moscow, the city council decided to privatize the ownership of residences. However, instead of selling them—which would have provided the USSR with the ability to increase production and purchasing by increasing the incentives for Soviets to work harder so that they could afford to buy a home—they decided to award them scot-free to the current residents, on the social ground that they suffered enough.)

My argument is not that economic considerations in these and other cases should have been given precedent. On the contrary, as I have shown in *The Moral Dimension* (1988), all people find some mix that is appropriate to them between their values and their economic needs. The United States is also far from a free market, a country of raw capitalism, because its economy is guided by many social considerations reflected in Medicare, Social Security, unemployment insurance, and numerous other measures.

To urge post-Communist societies to shift to raw capitalism is to ignore the inherent social instability (which led all Western countries to welfare capitalism) of such a system, and to invite social tensions that are explosive and will contribute to removing both democratic institutions and the drive to capitalism. These societies need time and encouragement to find their own balance between whatever social values are dear to them and economic efficiency. To view their rejection of Communist tyranny as an unmitigated taste for raw capitalism is to misunderstand their social orientation and render their transitions much more difficult, if not outright impossible.

According to Harvard sociologist Orlando Patterson, Westerners should not assume that people will automatically embrace democracy. To us, the concept of freedom is so basic that we overlook the fact that most cultures have rejected the whole idea.[46]

In January 1992 the IMF was pushing President Boris Yeltsin of Russia to raise petroleum prices ten to fifteen times over their current levels (they had already been quadrupled). Such a rise would put the cost of heating oil beyond the reach of many people.[47] Unlike Southern California, heating in Russia is a most elementary necessity. The question that the Russians must ponder is: Do they wish to put items that are needed to sustain life beyond the reach of many people?

External Factors

All that has been suggested above must be "corrected" by taking into account external factors that can increase or decrease the levels of friction and associated stress in the cases of socio-economic transition at hand. There is, however, a tendency to exaggerate what can be accomplished by foreign aid and forgiveness of debt. When an economy is very large, like that of Russia, and external help is proportionally puny, the ability to ease the transition is particularly small. Even for a country the size of Poland, external help is likely to be far from sufficient to make rapid transition tolerable. This is the case, in part, because some matters cannot be rushed (e.g., retraining of workers, building roads, modernizing ports) and because aid tends to be used for immediate ameliorative purposes such as buying food (as Poland did in the 1970's), which in the long run builds up demand but no productive capacity. Thus, the political gain (of sustaining the regime) is temporary. Even in a smaller economy (eastern

Germany, population, 17 million, or Poland; population, 38 million) with a practically unlimited commitment of resources and skills, as well as the infusion of Western values (as is the case in Germany), the transition, though somewhat more hurried, proves to be much more difficult and exacting than had been widely expected. "Henry Maier, a professor at the University of Flensburg and an expert on eastern German economics, said the Government had failed to grasp the immensity of the problems in shifting an industrial economy from socialist central planning to free-market capitalism. 'The Government had the naive notion that the free market would take care of everything,' Mr. Maier said, 'Instead, it has been a disaster.'"[48]

As predicted, the resulting stress already threatens Polish democracy, such as it is.

Tadeusz Kowalik writes in *Dissent*:

> I do not deny that [Finance Minister] Balcerowicz and Sachs have had some success in stabilizing the economy, particularly market relations, in moving from a situation of acute shortages to one in which a startling array of consumer goods is available, and in reducing the rate of inflation (although it remains so high that the premier himself has referred to it as insane). But as a procedure intended to change the economic system "shock therapy" has proved a disaster. Whatever its achievements, they are dwarfed by the enormous social costs. The process was supposed to be something like Schumpeter's "creative destruction": short-lived crisis and recession were supposed to create the conditions for modernization, increased innovation, and so on. But what do we have? We have mass unemployment (more that 1.2 million), and it is expected to increase. Despite this, labor discipline has barely improved, and improvement in quality of output is virtually imperceptible. Not only has so-called hidden employment not declined—and this was supposed to be one of the chief aims of the whole operation—but, relative to industrial output, it has actually increased (industrial output has fallen by 24 percent and now is 40 percent lower than at the end of 1989, employment by 11 percent). This means that unit costs have increased considerably and that the economy has become even more inefficient.

> The process of "creative destruction" has turned out to be lopsided: plenty of destruction but so far little creativity.[49]

In 1991 President Lech Walesa was barely prevented from suspending much of the meager democracy Poland has evolved. On several occasions he suggested suspending the power of Parliament on key economic issues and allowing him to govern by decree. He frequently refers to a need for "decisive, even 'dictator-like' leadership in economic matters."[50] He stated that "there's no place for democracy when you are driving a bus."[51]. So far, Parliament has been able to withstand his pressure.[52] There are also growing threats to the stability of the regime from strikers and demonstrations. In Russia and the republics as well, many fear that the shock therapy, too late and poorly planned, is likely to lead to food riots, social disorder, and disillusionment with democracy and a market economy.[53]

When all is said and done, the transition to post-Communist societies shows that friction is generally high. It's study provides a list of the factors that slow down the process, which are familiar from other less developed economies. The inability to modify most of these factors in quick order has clear policy implications. The main one is that external pressures to rush transitions will cause them to be aborted (as the pain and costs of transition exceed the public tolerance, at least within democracy). It also suggests that foreign aid is best disbursed at a low level for the long run than massively for the short run. (Those who argue that our political system is unable to sustain such commitments should examine the long-term commitments of aid that the United States has maintained to Israel, Egypt, Turkey, and Korea. True, particular mixes of national security considerations and ethnic pressure played a role in these cases, but aid to Poland has its own ethnic base and there are at least as good security reasons to support transition to post-communism as there are to support Egypt.)[54]

The Unevenly Paced Clocks and Political Commitment

Aside from the generally high level of friction, difficulties for socio-economic transitions are caused by what might be called the problem of the unevenly paced clocks. That is, some socio-economic processes are inherently more friction-laden than others. To the extent that changes must be multifaceted (which all major societal, economic, and political changes are), pushing the relatively quicker processes to proceed at full speed, they generate major imbalances because the other processes cannot keep up.

At issue in particular is the respective pace of three kinds of processes. The first are those that can proceed at a relatively rapid pace: deconstructive acts such as closing down state plants and collective farms, deregulation, slashing of subsidies, and removing currency controls. Much slower in pace are the processes of reconstruction, such as the opening of new plants, development of the infrastructure, and retraining of the labor force. The fastest and most volatile are expectations. Expectations are a social-psychological variable that neoclassical economists often assume they can model, but it is actually one of the least understood factors, precisely because it is highly volatile and driven largely by social and psychological factors and not by economic ones. It seems that one of the few things we can say with certainty about expectations is that they move with less friction than most processes. Thus, very shortly after the beginning of the transition from communism, expectations shot up, with Poles expecting democratization to result in quick prosperity and a Western lifestyle. When this did not follow in short order, the mood soured, resulting in the rejection of the Mazowiecki government in November 1990 and disinterest in the October 1991 elections.[55]

Although the knowledge of how to keep expectations realistic is far from established, certainly policies of oversell further fan inflated expectations rather than help keep them closer to reality and more frustration-proof. During a 1990 visit to Poland, a social scientist colleague pointed to my published statement that such expectations were unrealistically high, by stating that "we are very pessimistic, indeed maybe too much. We do not expect to catch up with the West before the end of the century." At the time, the Polish income per capita was a fourth of that of Greece, roughly $1,750 per capita. Expecting the Gross National Product (GNP) to increase fourfold was an extremely optimistic projection. For comparison's sake, the United States doubled its income only once every generation, under much more favorable circumstances.

Neoclassical economists sometimes add privately that a main reason they favor rapid transitions is that they fear a lack of political commitment to a long-term, more gradual transition. If, however, we are correct that rapid transition cannot be accomplished, one must ask under what conditions a more gradual transition could be attained. The answer seems to be: (1) if one could keep expectations low, so that results would be fulfilling rather than frustrating; (2) if the rewards of the transition could be kept high compared to the pain that a "pull" strategy (see below) seems to offer; and (3) if the moral case for the new regime could be strongly made, which is easier to do for a more humane and less brutal transition.

One way to ensure that the slower paced processes, after they have been hurried all they can be, will set the pace for the total socio-economic change is to build on a "pull" instead of "push" strategy. In post-Communist Poland this has been suggested in the form of not closing profitable state enterprises, but providing favorable terms (say, of credit) to the new, private ones and allowing those, as they grow, to pull labor and other resources (to the extent that they can be salvaged) away from state ones, which will then die on the vine.

The term "profitable state enterprises" may be surprising on two accounts. First, can they be? Second, if they are, why close them? Poland's midsize car industry is useful to illustrate the point. In 1990, after state enterprises were forced to work under commercial conditions (e.g., their subsidies abolished), the said auto industry was quite profitable, because although it made fewer cars, it could increase prices because of its monopoly status and the high demand for cars. The champions of the rush to the free market nevertheless planned to close the factories (before the November 1990 elections) because they were state-owned and because they were less efficient than Western ones. According to one economist, Polish workers were making about three cars per year each, compared to ten cars per worker at Chrysler. It was suggested that plants be privatized or their monopoly status be attacked by increasing car imports, even if that would use up scarce foreign currency. However, privatization was delayed because, among other reasons, no investors could be found to take over, and mere privatization would not have increased efficiency because, among other things, Chrysler has a much higher capital outlay per worker than the Polish plants. While it is true that competition with Western carmakers could have been achieved "right away" by opening the border, the result would have been mainly a decline in Polish production of cars, without any pickup elsewhere. Hence, in the short run, idling more resources, particularly workers, would not have increased output, but would have increased pain, costs, and social stress. If private Polish industries, say, animation, were given time to grow and expand, they would have drawn workers from the no-longer-subsidized state industries. As long as the "pulling" industries determined the pace, rather than those being shut, there would be much less transitional imbalance and resulting economic, human, and political strain.

Conclusion

Friction (psychological, sociological, political) is a major social science variable. The beginning assumption in socio-economics should be that friction is high for most changes. The perils of disregarding this generalization is illustrated by examining the transition from command-and-control economies to freer ones.

Notes

1. *The National Interest* 19 (Spring 1990):95–102; *The New York Times*, June 17, 1990; *Challenge*, July-August 1991, 4–10.
2. For additional discussion, see Amitai Etzioni, *The Moral Dimension: Toward a New Economics* (New York: The Free Press, 1988), chap. 6.
3. *Christian Science Monitor*, March 1, 1990.
4. *The New Yorker*, November 11, 1989, 89. For more information on Sachs's proposals, see Jeffrey Sachs and David Lipton, "Poland's Economic Reform," *Foreign Affairs* 69 (Summer 1990):47–66; "Creating a Market Economy in Eastern Europe: The Case of Poland," *Brookings Papers on Economic Activity* 1(1990):75–147; "Privatization in Eastern Europe: The Case of Poland," *Brookings Papers on Economic Activity* 2(1990):293–341.
5. *The New York Times*, November 10, 1990.
6. *Business Week*, November 11, 1990.
7. Sylvia Nasar, "Russians Are Urged To Act Fast," *The New York Times*, January 6, 1992, D1.
8. Stephen Engelberg, "Will Russia Find Lessons in Poland's Shock Therapy?" *The New York Times*, January 12, 1992, E4.
9. *The New York Times*, June 17, 1990.
10. *The Washington Post*, November 27, 1990.
11. *The New York Times*, December 31, 1989.
12. *The New Yorker*, November 13, 1989, 90.
13. *The Wall Street Journal*, June 29, 1990, A10.
14. *The New York Times*, February 13, 1991, A1.
15. *The New York Times*, January 10, 1992.
16. *The Independent*, November 2, 1990, 21.
17. *The New York Times*, March 3, 1990, A1.
18. *The New York Times*, June 17, 1990, F13.
19. Valtr Komarek, "Shock Therapy and Its Victims," *The New York Times*, January 5, 1992, E13.
20. *The New York Times*, July 24, 1990, A8.
21. Private Communication, 1991.
22. For additional discussion on the management problems in Eastern Europe and its effects on Western investments, see K. J. Blois, "Eastern Europe's Problems—Are Western Management Approaches Applicable Yet?" *Eastern Business Journal* 6 (1991):184–88.
23. *The New York Times*, November 12, 1991.
24. *The Wall Street Journal*, December 3, 1991.
25. Interviewed by Agnieszka Wroblewska, *Zycie Warsawy*, November 22, 1990.
26. Private communication, 1990.
27. *The New York Times*, April 9, 1990, D5.
28. *The Washington Post*, March 10, 1991, H1.
29. *The Wall Street Journal*, June 29, 1990, A10.

30. *The New York Times*, May 25, 1990, A10.
31. *The New York Times*, February 13, 1991, A1.
32. *The New York Times*, January 10, 1992.
33. On the first point, see James S. Duesenberry, *Income, Saving, and the Theory of Consumer Behavior* (Cambridge, MA: Harvard University Press, 1952); on the second, Daniel Kahneman, Paul Slovic, and Amos Tversky, *Judgment Under Uncertainty: Heuristics and Biases* (Cambridge: Cambridge University Press 1982).
34. *The Washington Post*, November 24, 1991.
35. *The New York Times*, January 3, 1992.
36. Quoted in the *Christian Science Monitor*, August 7, 1990, 7. For more on economic conversion, see *Economic Adjustment and Conversion of Defense Industries*, John Lynch, ed., (Boulder, CO: Westview Press, 1987).
37. Amitai Etzioni, *An Immodest Agenda* (New York: McGraw-Hill, 1983).
38. *Business Week*, November 20, 1989.
39. *The Washington Post*, May 9, 1990, A22.
40. *The New York Times*, May 12, 1990, A8.
41. *The New York Times*, February 5, 1990.
42. *The Washington Post*, January 23, 1990, D1.
43. *The New York Times*, October 29, 1990, D4.
44. *The Wall Street Journal*, October 16, 1991.
45. *Los Angeles Times*, May 2, 1988.
46. Orlando Patterson, *Freedom in the Making of Western Culture* (New York: Basic Books, 1991).
47. *The New York Times*, January 11, 1992.
48. *The New York Times*, February 13, 1991, A1. For a detailed account of transition difficulties in Berlin, see "Letter From Berlin," *The New Yorker*, November 25, 1991, 55–108.
49. Tadeusz Kowalik, "The Costs of 'Shock Therapy': Economic Transition in Poland," *Dissent*, Fall 1991, 499.
50. *The Washington Post*, November 1, 1991.
51. Ibid.
52. See also *The New York Times*, October 30, 1991.
53. *The Washington Post*, January 2, 1992.
54. For more information on the transitions of Communist regimes, see Antoni Z. Kaminski, *An Institutional Theory of Communist Regimes: Design, Function, and Breakdown* (San Francisco: Institute for Contemporary Studies, 1992).
55. *The New York Times*, October 29, 1991.

2

American Competitiveness:
The Moral Dimension

At first glance, America's loss of competitiveness seems a simple matter. The litany is all too familiar: We are doing less well economically than we used to be; we are falling behind Germany and Japan and quite a few other countries; we are unable to pay for our worldwide military and other commitments (the so-called Paul Kennedy thesis). Single-cause explanations are readily offered. The deficit of the federal government is too high, we do not save enough (and hence costs of capital in the United States are higher than in Japan), our schools produce an inferior labor force, and so on.

Actually, the situation is much more complex. By some measures we are doing quite well indeed, as recent books by Henry Nau and Joseph Nye have stressed.[1] By many criteria, we are much better off than Americans were a generation ago. There is little doubt than our children will have a significantly higher standard of living than we had (something few can be sure of in the post-Communist world and in many Third World countries). Desert Storm has shown that we can keep up a very impressive military might, using a relatively small proportion of the GNP. (Defense expenditures accounted for 5.7 percent of the GNP in 1989 as compared to 7.8 percent in 1970.)[2] Our universities are a mecca for the rest of the world. True, some other countries are moving forward faster by several measures, but they started from a much lower point. In any event, it seems unreasonable to expect that we can, or should, aspire to maintain the unique powerful status we had at the end of World War II, when Germany and Japan destroyed much of the other industrial nations (from the United Kingdom and France to the USSR), and we destroyed them, leaving us the only major economic power in the world. We deliberately (and, it seems, wisely) saw to it that the others got back on their feet.

And yet our inner sense correctly tells us that something is amiss. Before we can attend to these matters, a more precise characterization of the issues at hand is needed. In narrow economic terms, one matter that concerns us, as it ought, is the slowing of the GNP growth rate. During the Kennedy administration, the American economy grew more than 6 percent a year without overheating, with inflation around 1 percent. In the 1980's, the rate of inflation hovered around 4 percent, and the annual growth rate around 3 percent. These days our economy seems to be like an old locomotive: when it runs faster than about 2.5 percent of GNP growth, the economy overheats and the Federal Reserve uses recessionary breaks to cool it off by slowing it down. Low growth rates mean that we have relatively few new resources for all the additional goals we wish to advance, which makes us feel boxed in. When we see other nations, whose rate of growth (and hence flow of new resources) is much higher, we feel inadequate, inferior. We feel we have more than a touch of the British disease, another country whose growth rate is comparatively low and often seems demoralized.

But, deeper fear seems to gnaw at us. When our economic trends are down (not in terms of absolute income but of growth) and that of others are up, the possibility that we shall fall ever more behind, indeed, may crumble, becomes very real. Others will be able to buy ever more of our companies and country, become the centers of technological innovations, export, and so on. We fear that rather than settle into a comfortable, slow but steady pace ("So what if others work harder and gain more?"), we shall continuously deteriorate, until we can no longer sustain a modern economy and our world role. We fear that we may become another Argentina, a country of high inflation and low productivity, rattled by great social strife (which often accompanies countries whose income growth slows, especially when it actually falls) and become an international pygmy. There is no assurance that such a fate will elude us.

More than matters of economy and national psyche are at stake. The underlying issues have strong social and moral elements that, in my judgment, both help explain the competitive challenge and point to part of the needed response.

Economics as Morality in Disguise

In large segments of our society, putting matters in outright moral terms is currently not fashionable. The trump of relativism is too powerful. Most times, when someone makes a moral point, the ready response is: "Well, that is in line with *your* set of beliefs, but according to some others. . .". Putting matters in economic terms lends them an aura of scientific neutrality and objectivity. Hence, instead of testifying before Congress, editorializing, and sermonizing that it is morally indecent for us to consume the fruits of the hard labor of our forefathers and mothers, which resulted in a rich economy, and leave little to our offspring—while saddling them with worldwide debts and a polluted, deteriorating environment short on many necessities from reliable sources of energy to drinkable water—we prefer to discuss the economic "dangers" of accumulating federal deficits, trade deficits, and low savings rates. And instead of arguing that it is unfair to collect a day's pay without putting in a day's work, we prefer to discuss lower productivity growth rates. Actually, the technical economic points are open to debate. For example, Japan has done and continues to quite well economically despite rather high deficits (e.g., in 1980 Japan's deficit accounted for 6 percent of its GNP; whereas in 1989, ours was 3 percent).[3] In any case, these technicalities do not answer the moral questions. Do we wish, even if it is economically feasible and not hazardous, to consume ever more and produce less, eat up our heritage and impoverish our children? I believe the answer is a resounding no, which is the moral imperative for the needed socio-economic reforms.

Our social/moral condition, as I see it, is best seen in historical context. For three generations (roughly from the 1820s to 1920s), America's first and foremost domestic dedication was to build up the means of production. In this age of industrialization, our GNP doubled every generation as we saved much and consumed relatively little. We also paid rather little heed to social needs, as we allowed industrialization to take priority over attending to most other social/moral concerns. (Child labor, the robber barons, and the shooting of strikers were some of the indications.) The Great Depression shifted our collective attention to some social needs, and World War II distracted us from domestic priorities. Only after World War II did we shift from raw to mature capitalism, partially attending to some social ills and launching an affluent, high-consumption society, as we assumed we had all the productive capacity a nation could wish to have and more. (We tend to forget that in the mid-1950's, our main concern was with finding uses for our affluence, and the danger we feared then was that as all consumer needs were sated, the economy, with its endless supply, would lack growth in demand, just about the opposite of our present predicament.) The fact and sense of affluence fed into an explosion of entitlements and widespread indulgence, the counterculture and ego-centeredness of the 1960's and 1970's. Why work hard or save? Why not consume all we can if we have found the secret of an unbounded cornucopia? In this affluent society, all restraints were questioned, authorities from doctors to scientists and from parents to presidents were delegitimated, and moral codes were eroded. Many Americans, not all and not equally, but large segments of society in varying degrees, engaged in a combined moral and economic permissiveness. Families came apart as more and more individuals sought to maximize themselves; the moral and character formation of the young was neglected; public schools deteriorated; work ethics declined; and public morality most assuredly did.

Moral and Socio-Economic Redevelopment

Assuming the preceding analysis is fairly accurate, America's economic problems—far from alarming, but disheartening to the psyche, stressful for the civic order, and potentially truly troubling—require an encompassing approach, one that sees economic matters within the social and moral context in which they are inevitably embedded. Reconstruction here entails at least the following elements:

The Family

A parenting deficit has resulted as the majority of mothers, even of young children, are leaving to work outside the household, joining the fathers who have always worked mainly outside the home. There has been a reverse flow into the household of a much smaller, often less qualified, labor force of babysitters, housekeepers, some grandparents, and undocumented workers. Parents often come home exhausted from a full day's work, still facing their household chores; in toto, children are often neglected, not so much in their custodial care (someone is usually, although by no means always, present to ensure that they won't run into the street, set the place on fire, and so on), but in their character formation and moral upbringing.

Traditionalists, who correctly perceive the problem, wish to treat it by insisting that women give up gainful employment and return to their roles of homemaker and mother. This seems to me unjust, because women and men have the same basic right to work outside the household, and unlikely. Nor is it satisfactory to exempt fathers from their parental responsibilities. Only a change in the total moral climate of the society, which is well on its way, will reduce the parenting deficit. Both parents will need to work less outside the household and dedicate more of their time to educating their young children.

How fathers and mothers share these responsibilities will have to be worked out by the couples themselves. Institutionalizing young children in child-care facilities, especially under the age of two, provides for inadequate bonding between the child and the parents at a critical formative age, in which other adults cannot effectively substitute for the parents, certainly not when they are as poorly paid as they typically are, which means that child-care workers are often among our least qualified employees. The more we articulate this social/moral message, the sooner the prestige scales will adjust: parenting of the young is vital; increasing one's purchasing power is not. Moreover, both the economy and the social order will benefit if the character formation of future generations is more successfully advanced.

Schools

Because, at best, parents will be slow to return to their duties at home, it must be expected that many children will continue to appear on the doorsteps of our schools socially and morally underdeveloped. Because we have more influence over what happens in schools than in families, we shall have to rely heavily on this second line of defense to ensure character formation of the young as a necessary precondition for their ability to acquire knowledge, learn skills, and become reliable employees and decent members of society. The secretary of education, Lamar Alexander, in his "revolutionary" educational reform plan, follows the ideas of several educational commissions that have recommended pumping more knowledge into American youngsters. They are to be given more math, science, and foreign languages, among other subjects. And to ensure that they are picking up the additional material, national tests are urged. These, together with increased parental choice (which allows parents to move their children—and taxpayers' funds —from one school to another), are to push schools to "shape up." The problem is that you cannot load, let alone increase the load, on a vessel until it is formed.

Plans to reform our schools overlook the fact that about half of our youngsters grow up in families that are not viable from an educational viewpoint. Frequent divorces, a bewildering rotation of boyfriends and girlfriends, and parents who come home from work exhausted both physically and mentally have left many homes with a tremendous parenting deficit. Instead of providing a stable home environment and the kind of close, loving supervision character formation requires, many child-care facilities, grandparents, and babysitters simply ensure that children will stay out of harm's way. As a result, personality traits essential for the acquisition of skills like math, English, and various vocational skills are often lacking. Children come to school without self-discipline, unable to defer gratification. Nor can they concentrate or mobilize themselves to the tasks at hand.

Many studies find students deficient in math and English skills. This does not even involve such advanced matters as whether students can craft a powerful essay or analyze a calculus problem. At issue is the ability to do simple arithmetic and write clear memos. Close examination of what is required points in one direction: the elementary knowledge involved can be taught quickly because it entails rather simple rules. The "rest" is a matter of self-discipline, adhering to the rules without jumping to conclusions.

Character formation has traditionally been viewed as a family matter, while the various commissions studying our nation's educational needs see schools as their purview. Also, deficiencies in areas such as reading comprehension are more readily measured and less controversial than character defects, such as the inability to delay gratification or to concentrate on tasks. Mainstream psychology has also been highly cognitive in its outlook. Since the 1960s, it has tended to deal with skills rather than personalities. Still, studies lend support to the thesis that one needs to prepare the students so they can acquire skills and specific knowledge.

One of the best bodies of data regarding character formation was collected by James Coleman and his colleagues at the University of

Chicago.[4] The data show that children who study well also have well-developed characters. The youngsters doing well in high-performance schools have two main attributes: they do quite a bit of homework and they relate positively to their schools. Homework is the giveaway cue: those who can do a great deal of it, largely unsupervised, have acquired self-discipline. And students need to respect their teachers and see their assignments as meaningful to sustain positive commitments to education.

Several other studies have reached similar conclusions. But the strongest evidence is found in the success of all-encompassing programs such as the Conservation Corps and some of the drug- treatment programs. These programs take youngsters who are often disoriented and lacking in motivation and skills and develop their psychic stamina and their ability to mobilize and make commitments. Then the acquisition of specific skills becomes relatively easy.

How may one enhance the much-neglected development of a child's character? It is important to start early. Companies would be serving their long-term interests by offering their employees (mothers and fathers) more leave in the first two years of a child's life. Parents ought to be advised that a premature emphasis on cognitive achievement and neglect of human development is self-defeating. One presupposes the other.

Recognizing that such a transformation in child-care policy is unlikely, and that many parents will probably continue to spend relatively little time developing their child's character, the schools must step in. Schools ought to start earlier, say, at age four, and be open longer during the day and into the summer to make up for some of the lost parenting.

Above all, schools must learn to examine their own culture the way corporations do. They will find that their greatest effect is not in what is lectured in classrooms but in the experiences they generate, the behavior their teachers model, and the attitudes they foster. Is the school taking education lightly, closing at any excuse, letting teachers come to class poorly prepared, or is it ardently committed to learning, the way many coaches are to winning? Are grades, a major source of recognition and reward, fairly allotted, or are they submitted late, with A's handed out easily to make teachers popular? Are the school's corridors, parking lots, and cafeterias a zoo, or are they places where one learns respect for others and civic order?

Last but not least, teaching in high schools since World War II has been specialized, which means that at the sound of the bell, every forty-five minutes or so, the student body is reshuffled among the various classrooms in which the specialized teachers (chemistry, math, Spanish) remain. As a result, it is difficult for bonds to form between teachers and groups of students, and peer bonds tend not to be classroom-based because students do not stay together as a group from one class to another. Because such bonding is important for teachers to be able to educate in the deeper sense of the term, above and beyond the transmission of skills, schools should be rearranged so that one teacher teaches three subjects (the best combination would be classes with high normative content, such as civics, history, and maybe literature) to the same group of students. This teacher would be the real "homeroom" teacher, responsible for fostering educational orientations and character formation in his or her students.

Beyond being a prerequisite for good study habits, self-discipline is essential in making an employee show up for work regularly, be responsible for the quality of his or her production, and take initiative. It is the basis of the work ethic, and it is an essential attribute for being a good community member who is tolerant of others and mindful of civic duties.

Community

We have come a long way from John F. Kennedy's challenge, "Don't ask what your country can do for you, but. . . , " to the age of "Give me!" We find that the majority of Americans wishes to slash big, bad government, but demands that its various services be increased. Cutting the deficit is on the lips of all, but few support higher taxes. The moral/economic tone of the times has been captured by a naive participant, who shot out during an audience participation TV show about the S&L mess: "The taxpayers should not have to pay for this; the government should!" In Washington, interest groups—most representing trade groups, industry, labor unions, and banks—advocate short-term economic interests, pushing the government to grant their members subsidies, tax exemptions, noncompetitive contracts, and loan guarantees. This reflects our recent propensity to take freely from the common till, but only very grudgingly to refill it. A new communitarian spirit of responsibility to the common good will have to grow (there are some early signs) to ensure that the essential societal balance between taking and contributing will be restored.

National Economic Policy (Not "Industrial")

Once the basic moral/social commitments and institutions are refurbished along the lines discussed, the underpinning will be readied to attend to the more specific, technical economic needs. Here there are two main opposing schools of thought that capture much of the public's and the policymakers' attention, while our economic salvation may actually lie in a middle course.

On the one side are the free marketeers. Clutching in their hand the works of Adam Smith, they firmly believe, as we know all too well, that if only the market would be left to its own devices, if regulation, taxes, limitation on international trade, and other government interventions were only removed, individual self-interest would propel the economy to ever-higher levels of accomplishment. Purists even oppose pressuring other countries to match our free-trade policy (if their governments wish to subsidize their products, we would be the beneficiaries, or so the argument goes), influencing the level of interest rates (by actions of the Federal Reserve), or trying to stabilize international exchange rates. In the 1980's and early 1990's we have moved in the direction of these policies, but our competitive problems and other economic ones have hardly receded.

On the other hand, there are those who favor industrial policy (usually those who also favor a big role for government in other matters). They point to Japan, especially to its Ministry of Trade and Industry, to suggest that we too need a government agency (the Department of Commerce is mentioned as a suitable candidate) that would determine which of our industries are obsolete (steel?) and which are the stars of the future (high tech?). Then a national development bank would shower the winners with easy credit, tax exemptions, and other governmental assistance, while the losers would be allowed to die on the vine. Critics point out that it is nearly impossible to tell the future winners from losers (the American textile industry was once written off and is now doing relatively well). They point out that our political system, which is largely driven by special-interest groups, will end up channeling funds to industries that have the most clout (often the old, established ones) rather than to the most promising ones (often the new, less powerful ones), and that the government intervention entailed is the source of the problem, not a solution.

The third policy approach, which I spelled out in my book *An Immodest Agenda*,[5] suggests that we ought to rely on the government to set the context for economic redevelopment, but not intervene in the specifics. For instance, we should set tax and credit policies that favor research and development, our engine of innovation, but avoid the system we have in basic research in which hundreds of committees pore over thousands of research applications to sort out whom the government will support and whom it will let be. We should expand IRAs, and more important, set aside the Social Security surplus to enhance the national level of saving, but not use our political system (which is indeed infested with interest groups) to finance select winners and punish losers. Let a generally higher level of resources reduce the costs of investments and let the market sort out the rest.

Above all, let the public authorities concern themselves with the reform of public schools along the lines discussed earlier and set a model of responsibilities by paying for what we spend, rather than further drawing down our heritage, mortgaging more of our future, and selling more of our assets.

Here we come full circle. In the end, no public economic policy will work, and the market by itself will not return us to a level of economic activity that can sustain our competitiveness, unless we get our moral and social house in order.

Notes

1. Henry Nau, *The Myth of America's Decline: Leading the World Economy into the 1990s* (New York: Oxford University Press, 1990); Joseph Nye, *Bound to Lead* (New York: Basic Books, 1990).
2. For the 1989 figure; Robert J. Samuelson, "The Peace Dividend," Newsweek, June 26, 1989, 56; for 1970, Editorial, *Air Force Magazine*, September 1990, 8.
3. For Japan's deficit in 1980; Gar Alperovitz and Jeff Faux, "Full Production, Local Stability," *The New York Times*, March 31, 1982, A31; for America's deficit in 1989; Peter Brimelow and Gregory Viscusi, "Socialism by Another Name," *Forbes*, December 9, 1991, 101.
4. James Coleman, Thomas Hoffer, and Sally Kilgore, *Private and Public Schools* (Chicago: National Opinion Research Center, 1981).
5. Amitai Etzioni, *An Immodest Agenda* (New York: McGraw-Hill, 1983).

3

Too Many Rights, Too Few Responsibilities

Sometimes a finding, while of limited significance by itself, illuminates a broader issue—perhaps even an encompassing, debilitating deficiency. One such finding is that young Americans expect to have the right to be tried before a jury of their peers, but are reluctant to participate in jury duty. This finding illustrates a more general societal imbalance: of a people that frequently opposes bigger government and higher taxes, but is anxious to expand or add governmental programs in many areas, from child care to national health insurance. And there are the many patriots who are proud of the U.S. show of force in the Persian Gulf, but who are simultaneously opposed to serving in the armed forces, or sending their sons and daughters to serve.

Some feel so strongly about the primacy of rights and so resentful of the implications of social responsibilities that they are blind to the peculiarity of the positions they advance. The American Civil Liberties Union (ACLU), for example, is opposed to searches in airports—the use of X-ray machines and metal detectors—which have significantly curtailed hijacking in the United States and reduced terrorism elsewhere.[1] That is, the ACLU opposes a measure that is minimally intrusive (i.e., only slightly diminishes, or, as we shall see, reinterprets one's rights to travel freely), but which significantly enhances public safety. In a similar vein, Dr. Theresa Crenshaw, a member of the President's Commission on the HIV Epidemic, found herself arguing against a common objection to AIDS testing, that "there is no point in having yourself tested because there is no cure."[2] This argument disregards the fatal effect on others who come into contact with the infected person. It is akin to saying that if a man exhales cyanide, there is no sense in telling him of his predicament as long as there is no cure for *him*. Other radical individualists oppose seat belts and motorcycle helmets, the war against drugs, and even such innocent voluntary measures as the fingerprinting of children to help cope with kidnapping.

Most Americans, however, are more reasonable. They are willing to accept *some limited* adjustments of their individual rights and some enhancements of their moral and public commitments in exchange for improved public safety, less drug abuse, enough order in the schools to permit teaching to take place, and to advance other compelling shared needs.

I choose the term adjustments to reflect, first of all, that limited changes are at issue, and second, to emphasize that what some consider a diminution of rights (which, however small in the eyes of some, is viewed by others as threatening our basic freedoms) is seen by still others as merely a reinterpretation of recent legal traditions. Thus, while some consider checkpoints on public roads to search for drugs a diminution of rights, others call such checkpoints a manifestation of what constitutes "reasonable search." (The Constitution bars "unreasonable searches," but what is "unreasonable" is subject to interpretation.) In either case, at issue is an adjustment in recent considerations of what is deemed legal and legitimate.

The public, it must be acknowledged, finds it difficult to deal in fine gradations, especially when the issues involved are highly emotional. There is, consequently, a danger that public concern may escalate and grow overzealous, supporting measures that are excessive and unnecessary to serve the social goals at hand. Hence, while this chapter focuses on those arguments advanced by radical individualists, specifically on those of their most industrious representative, the ACLU, I am even more troubled by the opposite extremists, authoritarians who would quarantine AIDS patients,[3] test every schoolchild for drugs,[4] and hang criminals from lampposts at random to curb violence and impose a tight moral order. Indeed, the quest for ways to adjust certain rights and the principles upon which such adjustments are to be based aims both at finding new ways to attend to compelling social needs *and* at helping prevent excessive reactions. While I am aware that media and society ask for ever more drama, I cannot state the need for moderation and careful action more strongly. We need to reset thermostats, not shatter windows or tear down walls.

To proceed gingerly, I deal first with the main objections raised against making any adjustments in the balance between individual rights and social responsibilities, and follow with specific criteria to guide how far to proceed without endangering constitutional foundations. At issue here are matters of privacy and recent interpretations of the Fourth Amendment—not modification of fundamental rights of much longer and stronger vintage, of the kind involved, say, if one were to curtail the First Amendment.

One last introductory comment: rights and responsibilities are, of course, much more encompassing than constitutional and even legal issues; they embrace matters of public morality and personal agendas. Here, however, the focus is limited to issues inherent in the debate over whether some constitutional rights need to be adjusted, because these matters in particular, as will soon become evident, get at the heart of the existing imbalance between excessive individual rights and insufficient social responsibility. Moreover, these issues illuminate the deep connections between constitutional questions and other aspects of public morality, social values, and civic virtue. In other words, although the question of rights and responsibilities may be discussed in the abstract or in sweeping philosophical terms, in effect, fortunately, the issues involved are actually manifest themselves in much less sweeping ways: Should there be mandatory drug testing for train engineers? Can we expel a disruptive student from a public school without a full-blown hearing? Should we require AIDS patients to disclose their sexual partners? Should *Miranda* rights be curbed?

Suspicion of Any and All Government Authority

Beneath the opposition by radical individualists to *all adjustments* of individual rights lies their deep-seated suspicion of all governmental authority, emanating from the days of authoritarian regimes. Gene Guerrero, an ACLU representative who opposes drug testing, cites Justice Brandeis:

> Experience should teach us to be most on guard to protect liberty when the Government's purposes are beneficent. Men born to freedom are naturally alert to repel invasion of their liberty by evil-minded rulers. The greatest dangers to liberty lurk in insidious encroachments by men of zeal, well-meaning but without understanding.[5]

However, if this viewpoint is applied to a functioning democratic government (if one plays on the fear that the nation might at any moment

be overturned by a totalitarian movement), then one comes to quite
untenable conclusions, including the refusal of any adjustment in constitutional rights, however compelling the social need. One ends up per-
ceiving constitutional rights not as a basis for sound government actions,
but merely as a protection *against* government.

This position is reflected in the ACLU opposition to mandatory
contact-tracing for those infected with AIDS:

> People fear that their confidentiality won't be protected because lists can be stolen
> and because, once the list exists, there can be no assurance that legislatures won't pass
> future laws permitting persons other than public health officials from having access
> to it. Once the government has a list of names, addresses, sexual preferences and other
> information about people who test positive for the AIDS virus and their partners . . .
> there is no way to guarantee that, whatever the confidentiality protections today,
> future laws won't be passed to allow insurers, school systems, or other state agencies
> to have access to such a list.[6]

By that logic, one can never act because it is quite true that it is never
possible to know with 100 percent accuracy what might occur at some
point in the future. True, it is necessary to be attentive at all times to
finding ways to bolster our freedoms—from providing civic education
(many Americans still need to be reminded of the virtues of various items
in the Bill of Rights) to imposing proper penalties on those who violate
the law by unauthorized disclosure of information in government files
(as has been done, by and large, with a high, although admittedly not a
perfect degree of success, by the IRS). However, leaks and other abuses
need not prevent us from calling upon government when faced with
compelling social needs, simply because at some unknown time, in some
unknown way, somebody might abuse the information it collects. To stay
with the example at hand, despite some serious abuses of IRS files by
the Nixon administration, there is little doubt that the country is better
off having such information on file. Without it, we could hardly finance
our social services or defense.

Yet the lengths to which one can be driven by suspicion is highlighted
by the opposition of the ACLU, following significant increases in the
kidnapping of children, to *voluntary* fingerprinting of children by some
schools,[7] so that if they are found years later they can be more readily
reunited with their parents (by easily proving that they are not the
kidnappers' children). Such fingerprinting also facilitates notification
when bodies are found; parents might otherwise look in vain for missing
children long after they had been buried in some pauper's grave.

The ACLU devotes a policy position to opposing the program. Why? Because of the "possibility" that the government might obtain access to the fingerprints. Their paper, "Children's Rights," reads: "Among the dangers posed by fingerprinting are the possibility of access by government agencies to fingerprinting records and dissemination of records, without the child's consent and without a warrant, either by consent of the child's parents or by subpoena."[8]

Furthermore, the ACLU's institutionalized paranoia leads it to believe that "fingerprinting tends to condition children and society to accept without protest unnecessary personal data collection and other invasions of privacy,"[9] which is sociological rubbish akin to saying that getting a driver's license or responding to the census will "condition" one to life in a police state.

This radical individualist position is a call for a paralysis with human and moral consequences, which may match, if not exceed, those of marginally modifying legal traditions, but which often directly invites grand disillusionment with the civic order. This, in turn, leads to calls to suspend the Constitution; to contaminate drugs to make their users "wretchedly ill";[10] to arm all citizen's with gun's so they can hunt down criminals à la Charles Bronson;[11] and to quarantine all HIV carriers.[12] If we are not to act out of fear that somehow an innocent law may one day lead to tyranny, we may well set forth the conditions that cause the kind and level of social distress that serves those who call for "strong" government. What we need is a lean, well-contained government, and not to proceed at every step on the assumption that no government act can be sanitized.

Some argue that the ACLU's (and other radical individualists') often dogmatic, if not extreme, positions are useful because they keep the amalgam of politics, the result of numerous tugs and pulls among many forces, more closely allied with individual rights than it would otherwise be if the ACLU and others were more reasonable or accommodating. Extremity in defense of virtue however, *is* a vice. Arguments advanced by radical individualists do cause harm because they are used by policy-makers and by courts to block programs that respond to compelling social needs. These arguments are not part of a healthy give-and-take in which their extreme nature is mitigated by the equally extreme positions of others. Rather than doctrines of excess, what is needed is cautious crafting of middle-of-the-road policies that take into account, according to criteria outlined below, ways to deal with social needs, while only minimally modifying individual rights—exactly the gentle mix the ACLU and its defenders, as we shall see, so effectively undermine.

The Slippery Slope

Probably the most common argument against suggested adjustments in the balance between individual rights and social responsibilities is a bogus piece of sociology, according to which, once someone seeks to modify a tradition, it crumbles—an argument often used by Orthodox Jews to oppose any changes in Judaism (e.g., seating men and women together in synagogue), and by traditional Catholics (e.g., conducting Mass in the vernacular). To use another analogy, it is widely held that moral order is precariously perched on top of a hill; if one so much as sets a foot on the edge of the slope, one will end up on one's rear end at the bottom of the heap.

Referring to the "dangers" of antismoking legislation, Barry Glassner, a fellow sociologist, takes the plunge: "If this pattern continues, we'll have a homogenized population in which everybody will be within the recommended weight ranges, and nobody will smoke anymore, and nobody will drink and everybody will work out."[13]

Another case in point: Over the years, most people have become accustomed to having themselves and their luggage searched at airports without much inconvenience. Yet the ACLU opposes airport security not only because it violates, they say, the Fourth Amendment, but also because of what they fear it may lead to: "Regrettably, we live in dangerous times. If the danger posed in one situation is thought to justify unconstitutional, emergency measures, where can the line be drawn? Today it is airports, tomorrow it may be banks or city streets."[14]

The argument is not *wholly* without merits. Once taboos are broken by a community tolerating a modification of its ethical code, it is not easy to find a stopping place. Those who challenged the traditional vows of fidelity in marriage often found it difficult to sustain their marital contracts and frequently ended up with no stable relationships at all. And "reform" in Judaism was followed (although it may well have occurred anyhow) by a massive flight from religious commitment. At the same time, it is equally evident that each time we collectively negotiate a step on the top of what are potentially slippery slopes, we do not end up at the bottom. Not every young woman who allows herself to be kissed (let alone goes further) before marriage ends up a hooker, as some of our forefathers and mothers warned, and not everyone who experiments with marijuana ends up a crack addict. Similarly, sex education has been introduced into many schools and has not lead, as arch-conservatives feared, to new heights of promiscuity, orgies, and the destruction of American society. That is, societies can reset their moral codes without necessarily losing their grip.

Intermediary Positions: Principles for Limited Adjustments

What is needed are principles that determine how far one travels in the new direction, steps on the slope to allow one to negotiate it without free fall. The criteria discussed next are, of necessity, examined one by one, though they must be used in conjunction.[15] That is, policies that qualify by the first measure still need to be examined by the second, third, and so on.

Clear and Present Danger

No adjustments should be implemented unless there is a clear and present danger—a real, readily verifiable, sizable social problem or need. Unfortunately, in a media-ized society, prophets of alarm rapidly gain wide audiences. There are frequent calls on policymakers and citizens alike to tighten their belts and modify their lifestyles, as well as calls for laws and constitutional protection to combat some imagined or anticipated scourge. For example, in the mid-1970's Americans were told that they must get out of cars and into mass transit because the United States was running out of oil. More recently, we are being told that America must introduce central planning in order to compete with the Japanese.

If policymakers and citizens would respond to all these cries of "wolf," society would frequently be put through the ringer, shaken and rearranged at great cost. Unfortunately, on most issues it is nearly impossible to discern well in advance which dangers are real and which are wildly exaggerated, if not outrightly false. Hence, one reluctantly reaches the humble conclusion that the best way is not to try to anticipate too far into the future (despite the obvious virtues of greater anticipation if it could be achieved with a fair level of reliability) and to embrace the humbler posture of not acting—especially in a grand way that involves major economic and human costs and diminutions of liberties—until there is a clear and present danger. Nuclear weapons, handguns, AIDS, and crack are clear and present. The evidence that they endanger large numbers of lives, if not the very societal existence, are incontestable. Killer bees do not, and the heating of the climate may also not warrant the kind of draconian measures several alarmists advocate as these lines are written in early 1992.[16] Other measures are justified because of the direct link between the cause and effect; if someone points a machine gun at a person's head, one has a right to take away the other's "property," even wrestle him or her to the ground, despite the fact that only one life may be at stake. The danger is clear and present. At the same time, we would condone, indeed penalize, the same conduct if one had only a suspicion that a gun owner might so use his or her weapon.

A specific case may help illustrate the issue at hand. The U.S. Department of Transportation maintained, after several train wrecks, that there was enough of a problem to warrant an adjustment that would allow random testing of train engineers for drugs and alcohol. Radical individualists opposed the policy for the usual reasons: only individualized case-by-case evidence of "probable cause" is proper grounds, and some measure of individualized suspicion is necessary for any type of drug or alcohol test.[17] In April 1991, the Ninth Circuit Court of Appeals upheld the Department of Transportation regulations that authorize truck and bus companies to drug-test their employees at random.[18] (The suit had been brought by labor groups claiming the regulations infringed on Fourth Amendment rights.) The Ninth Circuit Court had earlier upheld as constitutional the FAA's policy of random drug testing of airline employees.[19]

The following evidence suggests which data may be considered sufficient to show a direct link between drug and alcohol abuse and train wrecks. A 1979 study found that 23 percent of railroad operating employees were "problem drinkers," many of whom had been drunk on the job.[20] Of all the train accidents between 1975 and 1984, drugs or alcohol were "directly affecting" causes in forty-eight of them, accounting for thirty-seven fatalities and eighty injuries.[21] If anything, the danger seems only to have gotten worse. Out of 179 railroad accidents in 1987, the engineers in 39 of the cases tested positive for drugs, 34 percent more than in 1986.[22] In a January 1987 crash—in which 16 people died and 174 were injured when an Amtrak train was struck by a Conrail train—both the Conrail engineer and brakeman were later found to have been under the influence of marijuana.[23]

On August 28, 1991, a New York City subway motorman was speeding and derailed his train while switching from the express to the local track; the crash killed 5 passengers and injured more than 200. *Thirteen hours* after the crash, the motorman's blood alcohol level was 0.21 percent, twice the legal limit.[24] Coworkers reported seeing him have a few drinks on the job and smelled liquor on his breath. The leaders of the Transit Workers Union local decided after the accident to change the union's previous position against random testing, and accepted testing not only for drugs but for alcohol as well.[25]

While there are no simple mechanical numbers or criteria, it would seem that when 23 percent of the population is affected—that is, nearly one out of four—and when those involved deal *directly* with life and death (unlike the National Weather Bureau staff, which was also to be tested!), we would hold that random drug and alcohol testing is justified; this would apply not only to train engineers but to other high-risk groups, such as airline pilots. Once it is established that there is a clear and present danger, such matters must next be examined by the other criteria.

There is no alternative effective way to proceed without modifying the constitutional balance between individual rights and social responsibilities. Assume that we agree as a community that the human toll is such that we should discourage smoking (more than 300,000 people in the United States die from smoking annually),[26] especially among the young (as many as 95 percent of smokers were addicted before they were 21).[27] Moreover, we agree that the link between smoking and ill consequences is sufficiently tight for it to be considered a direct cause; hence, an adjustment is justified. (Robert Goodin points out additional moral justifications in an article on the ethics of smoking.[28]) Even if one accepts the radical individualist notion that people ought to be free to choose their purchases, even if self-injurious, smoking seems to harm others. Passive smoking accounts for approximately 2,400 cases of lung cancer per year, and in 1984 approximately 1,600 people died as a result of fires caused by smoking.[29] In addition, young preferences are not yet formed. Finally, most people reveal a slet to stop: according to a report of the Surgeon General in 1979, 90 percent of smokers have tried to quit.[30] (It would be different if we sought to impose, say, Buddhism onto Americans.)

Assumimg that these findings hold under further scrutiny (e.g., there are serious questions about the magnitude of secondary effects), they signify a clear and present danger; however, it does not yet follow that we need to make a constitutional adjustment. *We ought first to look for ways that require no or only little tampering with the Constitution.*

Armed with this criterion, we may conclude that raising the taxes on cigarettes is more justifiable than prohibiting cigarette ads. For one, the result is more efficient; a 10 percent increase in price is reported to correlate with a 12 percent decrease in demand.[31] Other studies corroborate this finding by demonstrating that young men's taste for cigarettes is highly controlled by their price.[32] On the other hand, while advertisements may convince some young people to take up smoking, it is widely agreed that their main effect is to shift people from one brand to another.

Second, and more to our point, curbing ads raises constitutional issues of freedom of speech, whereas raising taxes does not. Hence, even if curbing ads proved to be somewhat more efficient, raising taxes would still be preferable, as long as one could show that cigarette advertisements were not significantly more influential than prices.

Adjustments Should Be as Limited as Possible

Once it is established that there is no effective alternative to adjusting the constitutional balance between individual rights and social responsibilities (e.g., to prevent the harms of secondary smoke and to avoid imposing the health-care costs caused by smoking on society), *we must look for options that will make the most minimal intrusion possible, rather than proceeding with a sledgehammer.*

An examination of the debate over *Miranda* provides a good example of how one may find ways to trim rather than pound. In recent years, *Miranda* has come under criticism as excessively favoring criminals. The extent to which *Miranda* actually hobbles the police and prosecutors is a much-debated and scrutinized topic warranting long study just to sort out this question. Also, it is difficult to tell readily whether recent court rulings have already sharply or only moderately affected the reach of *Miranda*—although most would agree that over the past ten years, the balance has tilted somewhat toward fewer rights for criminals and greater public safety. Our concern here is to illustrate what a reasonable intermediary position looks like, rather than settling many attending intricacies.

At one extreme is the radical individualist position that no changes are to be made whatsoever, as if a rather recent legal tradition, not in effect until 1966, had the standing of the Bill of Rights and the sanction of the Founding Fathers. On the other hand, authoritarians argue that many rights accord criminals more constitutional protection than is afforded their victims. Former attorney general Meese wanted to do away with *Miranda* altogether because, he said, "it provides incentives for the suspects not to talk" and "only helps guilty defendants."[33] The Office of Legal Policy of the Justice Department under the Reagan administration issued a position paper that called for a wholesale overturning of the *Miranda* decision.[34]

A reasonable intermediary position seems to be to *let evidence stand even when it was collected despite a technical error*, as long as there is no indication of bad faith, making sure to include an indication of the error in the relevant personnel file at the appropriate law-enforcement agency to avoid repetitions. This was achieved in a 1985 Supreme Court case, in which a suspect confessed to a crime before he was read his *Miranda* rights, was later informed of his rights, and then confessed again. The Court unanimously agreed that the first confession could not be used as evidence, even if it had been given voluntarily and without coercion; but it ruled 6 to 3 that the unsolicited admission of guilt did not taint the second confession so that it must also be excluded.[35] In a similar decision, the Supreme Court ruled in 1987 that the police are not required to tell the suspect about each crime for which he or she may be questioned because, Justice Lewis Powell wrote, *Miranda* specifically requires that "the police inform a suspect that he has the right to remain silent and that *anything* he says may be used against him."[36]

Another example of a carefully honed adjustment, not from the *Miranda* area, is the introduction of some restrictions on the inadmissibility of evidence uncovered during discovery that was technically flawed. In 1984 a police officer believed that in a given house a murderer had left the instrument of his crime. Since it was a Sunday afternoon and the local court was closed, the officer called on a judge at his home. The officer presented the judge with an application for a search warrant accompanied by an affidavit showing sufficient reason for the request (as required by the Fourth Amendment). The judge fully agreed that the "probable cause" needed for a legal search was present and indicated his approval on a form, as is routinely done. The officer indeed found the murder instrument. When the perpetrator was brought before the court, however, the defense argued that there was no legal warrant—because the judge had mistakenly filled out the form inappropriately (it referred to drug paraphenalia rather than a murder instrument, but the police confined their search to the items indicated in the affidavit). The lower court wanted to let the killer walk, but the Supreme Court ruled that the incriminating evidence gathered by the police should not be excluded on the basis of the judge's technical mistake because the officers had relied on the warrant in good faith.[37]

The debate over the rights of students provides still another example of a reasonable intermediary position. Many observers agree that both substantive rights of students in public schools and their due process rights have reached a level that has made it difficult for public schools to function. Linda Bruin, the legal counsel for the Michigan Association of School Boards writes, "Following the split decision in *Goss v. Lopez*, 419 U.S. 565 (1975), which struck down an Ohio statute permitting student suspensions from school without a hearing, educators expressed fears that they no longer would be able to discipline students efficiently."[38] The subject is complicated by the fact that, as they stand, procedures vary from state to state. Some already have in place what seem to be reasonable adjustments; others need to follow.

What is an intermediary position between according students full-fledged Fourth Amendment rights, in effect deterring teachers and principals from suspending them, and declaring students fair game to any capricious school authority? It seems reasonable that students who are subject to expulsion and suspension should be granted due process to the extent that they are notified of the nature of their misconduct and given an opportunity to respond; both actions must occur before the expulsion takes place. Still, expulsion need not guarantee students the right of counsel nor need it warrant calling and cross-examining witnesses, because this would unduly impede the ability of schools to maintain an educational environment. Moreoever, schools are allowed to maintain, for internal purposes, additional restrictions and simplified procedures because they are meant to be small communities, rather than adversary environments. Far from a novel approach, several state courts have already been modifying school policies in the directions we suggest.[39]

To reduce the danger of slipping down the slope, it is important to draw additional moral and legal "notches" along the way to prevent slippage. Thus, while it is appropriate for students charged with expulsion to call upon their rights to due process, they need not be provided the same opportunities when they wish to protest their grade in a class. Radical individualists are strongly opposed to any modification of due process and to searches and seizures and drug tests without providing, before the fact, case-by-case plausible evidence to a third party (an independent judge) that the action called for is justified.[40] Authoritarians would suspend such constitutional protections to "win the war on drugs." Some who, like the author, seek intermediate principled "notches" find that one can make a strong case that random searches of automobiles on public highways are significantly different from random searches of homes.[41] Autos are an optional means of transportation, convey passengers on public territory, and travel in places where behavior under the influence of drugs may affect others; homes are true castles, truly private, and what we do in them is much less likely to harm others.

Another reasonable measure is to require people who drive into open-air drug markets to show their driver's license and car registration. This situation arose in Inkster, a small community just outside Detroit, where the drug trade was so furious that the local residents could rarely take to the streets and lived in constant fear of their lives and the corruption of their children. The county sheriff set up roadblocks from midnight to 6:00 A.M. each night to check drivers' licenses and registrations. The tactic broke up the open drug market. But it had to be stopped when the ACLU intervened and a court accepted its arguments.[42]

Another option to abate open-air drug trafficking is the ordinance passed in Alexandria, Virginia, that allows police to arrest those who are loitering for the purpose of engaging in an unlawful drug transaction.[43] Unlike old loitering laws, which were used by the police to harass minorities, the new "loitering plus" statutes are designed to prevent such violations by defining specific conditions that must be met before an arrest can be made. In Alexandria, there are seven such prerequisites: among them are that the person must be on the street in a drug-trafficking area for more than fifteen minutes and during this time he or she must have face-to-face contact with more than one person involving actions that indicate that a concealed object is to be exchanged.[44]

One may devise new measures designed to reduce the constitutional impact of the suggested adjustments. The Supreme Court, in June 1990, approved roadside sobriety checkpoints, which the ACLU had successfully opposed in several states. The checkpoints, the Supreme Court majority argued, are minimally intrusive and last less than thirty seconds. Going one step further, the "intrusion" of the checkpoints is diminished even more if the authorities systematically and repeatedly inform drivers that such checkpoints are being operated, without disclosing their precise locations. Such warnings do not detract from their efficiency, but they make them less threatening to legal traditions: once the potential of a search on a given road has been posted, travel thereon can be construed as implied consent. (True, the courts have ruled that a person's agreement to be subject to unreasonable procedures is not valid, even if given before the fact; however, *these* checkpoints are reasonable.) Likewise, job requirements for all new train engineers, air traffic controllers, police officers, and other workers whose professions entail high risk to the public may include consent to be subject to drug and alcohol tests (older workers may be given a year's time to relocate if they refuse to accept the new requirement).

Aside from legal considerations, there are matters concerning the practical burdens involved. For example, courts may correctly object to sobriety test points that create major traffic jams and may insist that there be safe places for drivers to pull off the road and that they be given adequate warning about the procedure. Indeed, the fact that these tests last less than a half-minute is in their favor; so is the short delay that airport searches impose. The objection that urine tests are highly intrusive, that, as Justice Anthony Kennedy said, they invade "an excretory function traditionally shielded by great privacy,"[45] is quite compelling, as is the fact that the roadblocks in Michigan and highway sobriety checks are *less* invasive.

While it is both useful and convenient to distinguish between legal and practical considerations, it should be noted that they are intertwined. To wit, practical burdens could arise to a point that they become a form of government harassment, which is one of the main infractions from which the Bill of Rights is meant to shield us.

In short, far from yielding to demands to gun down any private airplane or speedboat that approaches a U.S. border unidentified, break down the doors of people's homes at midnight, or quarantine all HIV-positive persons to combat drugs and AIDS, we see justification to introduce many measures that are minimally intrusive, in either legal or practical terms, whatever the purists fear. Thus, sobriety checkpoints; searches of cars on public roads; roadblocks on roads leading to open-air drug markets; testing of train engineers, pilots, air traffic controllers, and other individuals whose jobs entail high risk to others; and requiring AIDS patients to disclose sexual partners, if the precautions indicated are taken, are both overdue and legitimate.

Efforts Should Minimize or Avoid Side Effects

Aside from checking policies against the said criteria, one should also take pains to reduce deleterious offshoots of a given policy. For example, AIDS testing and contact tracing can lead to a person losing his or her job and health insurance if confidentiality is not maintained. Hence, any introduction of such a program should be accompanied by a thorough review of control of access to lists of names of those tested, procedures used in contacting sexual partners, professional education programs on the need for confidentiality, and penalties for unauthorized disclosure and especially for those who discriminate against AIDS patients or HIV carriers. All this may seem quite cumbersome, but in view of the great danger that AIDS poses for individuals and its high cost to society, these measures are clearly appropriate.

A good example of a program that has kept negative side effects to a minimum and, as a result, enhanced its own acceptability, is the use of airport X-ray machines and metal detectors. These procedures allow airport security to confiscate concealed weapons that could otherwise be brought on board and thus help to prevent hijackings. Such searches are deliberately *not* used to stop drug trafficking and other crimes.

The Misuse of Efficiency

An examination of numerous writings, court briefs, and congressional testimony of radical individualists reveals a common pattern: much more attention is paid to the alleged inefficiencies of the suggested policy modifications than to their constitutional and moral legitimacy. This is surprising, because the opponents of suggested adjustments are, as a rule, not particularly schooled or trained in technical evaluation of the policies involved and do not care to find new or remodeled government "inter-ventions" that work effectively. It would seem that their underlying motivation is not a genuine quest for efficiency and cost-benefit assess-ment—an examination that definitely has its place next to (and in addition to) moral/constitutional evaluation. Obviously, if one can show that a planned step or program cannot work (or worse, that it is counterproduc-tive), it is a compelling way to lay it to rest—far more so than arguing that some interpretation of the Fourth Amendment is more important than, say, preventing drunk and stoned train engineers from derailing trains or removing guns from the schools.

The misuse, indeed, disingenuous use, of the efficiency argument on the part of the ACLU and others is evident in several ways. First, when radical individualists evaluate suggested government interventions, whatever they are and from whatever numerous perspectives they are assessed, these groups almost always conclude thatthe proposals are unreasonable, unproductive, ineffectual, and inefficient. Yet they reach such conclusions without any scientific attempt to collect facts and interpret them systematically and fairly. Instead, facts are picked and interwoven to shape a "case," like lawyers do when they are filing a brief, rather than the way scholars or scientists would proceed.

A typical example is an ACLU position paper that evaluates "manda-tory contact tracing" of AIDS patients in seven ways and finds no merits, only deficiencies.[46] First, the ACLU claims that contact tracing would drive people away from voluntary testing sites, and hence would have an opposite, counterproductive effect. No evidence is given, only conjec-ture; the question of whether the policy is efficient on the grounds that while some would be driven away, others would be helped to stop infecting still others is not examined.

Next, the ACLU argues that "contact tracing depends on the cooper-ation of the tested person."[47] It is argued that "requiring" disclosure is meaningless, that it is "no more likely to achieve its ultimate goal of notification than a voluntary model."[48] No evidence is given, and the total experience of sanctioning by law (i.e., the fact that the fear of sanction is a factor in one's decision making), the expressive role of law (it captures and communicates our values), and the interactive effect be-tween law and voluntary morality (we tend to do what is right in part so nobody will make us do it) are all ignored.

Evidence that mandatory testing will drive people away is taken from a highly speculative story that appeared in the *Chicago Tribune* which dealt with the first days of such a program in Chicago, before people had a chance to discover the extent to which its confidentiality was maintained.[49] In another case, the ACLU cites a statement by Senator Jesse Helms as evidence of potential government acts: "Senator Helms admitted on CBS's 'Face the Nation' that the reason to collect names is ultimately so the government can isolate those who are positive."[50] In yet another ACLU position paper, the standards that AIDS tests must meet to be deemed acceptable are set so high that none of them could qualify. Moreover, the paper calls AIDS testing worthless because "there is as yet no way to cure HIV or to render it incommunicable."[51]

Finally, it is evident that even if somehow the said interventions could be made or would turn out to be efficient, radical individualists would continue to oppose them as vehemently as before. For example, a major argument against testing train engineers for drugs, even after a wreck, is that the presence of drugs is said not to be evidence of impairment. However, the same radical individualists also oppose sobriety tests, despite the fact that the presence of alcohol above a certain level certainly does impair performance and judgment. Similarly, the ACLU states:

> Even if there was empirical evidence indicating that *Miranda* had impeded law enforcement, this would be an insufficient basis to overturn the decision. . . . Thus, even though the OLP's [Office of Legal Policy] evidence of a negative impact on law enforcement is extraordinarily weak, its argument for overturning *Miranda* would have to be rejected even if the argument were based on stronger evidence.[52]

So the underlying structure of many of these arguments is "Let's argue for inefficiency, but if it turns out to be efficient, let's oppose it anyhow."[53]

In short, one would surely not favor even a small adjustment in the balance between individual rights and social responsibilities (in favor of, say, public safety) if a policy were inefficient; nor would even a major gain in efficiency justify setting aside a major constitutional tenet. But when a policy can be shown to be effective and the adjustment can be limited, this is a direction in which we ought to go. The Constitution is a living creation: it has been and will continue to be adjusted to new facts of life, although it needs to be fine-tuned with great caution and care, and never wantonly.

Conclusion

The world is not on fire, although those caught in the cross fire of gangs in some parts of Los Angeles or between drug dealers in the nation's capital may think otherwise. Hence, cries to set aside constitutional protections to "win the war" against drugs or any other enemy are clearly not justified. However, because additional deteriorations of the civic order may play into the hands of alarmists, and because the social needs they call attention to do constitute clear and present dangers, we must act. Business as usual will not do. The purists, who wish to stick to their favorite interpretations of constitutional rights and not give an inch, do not allow us to adjust to the new societal realities.

Obviously, much that needs to be done has to take place in other societal realms, such as reforming schools and fostering an economy that is able to provide more meaningful jobs to youngsters in ghettos. The moral climate is significant, however, as is its expression in laws. To help shore up the civic order, Americans will need to adjust *some* of their cherished rights, such as traveling encumbered, and those who work in high-risk jobs may be required to be tested for drugs. Some will have to disclose the names of their sexual contacts or take other such measures. Working out the details of what needs to be done may seem complicated and cumbersome, and it may well not be dramatic enough to play on the evening news. Given the fragile nature of all freedoms, though, adjustments should be made gingerly rather than sweepingly. Nevertheless, they can no longer be much delayed if civic order is to be shored up.

Notes

1. "Airport Searches," Policy #270, American Civil Liberties Union, 359.
2. Theresa L. Crenshaw, "HIV Testing: Voluntary, Mandatory, or Routine?" *The Humanist*, January-February 1988, 31.
3. See Ronald Bayer, *Private Acts, Social Consequences: AIDS and the Politics of Health* (New York: The Free Press, 1989); Stephen C. Joseph, "Quarantine: Sometimes a Duty," *The New York Times*, February 10, 1990.
4. John Lofton, "Drug Tests for Kids Teach the Right Lesson," *USA Today*, January 1, 1990.
5. Gene Guerrero, speech before the American Society of Industrial Security, November 8, 1989.
6. "Mandatory Name Reporting," a report of the AIDS and Civil Liberties Project, American Civil Liberties Union Foundation, 2.
7. "Children's Rights," Policy #272, ACLU, 363.
8. Ibid.

9. Ibid., 364.
10. Paul Weyrich, "Conservatism for the People," *National Review*, September 3, 1990, 27.
11. Walter E. Williams, "The Cost of Crime Has Fallen," *Conservative Chronicle*, November 7, 1990, 29.
12. Joseph, "Quarantine"
13. See Glen Evans, "Stub Out Antismoking Zealotry," *The New York Times*, May 27, 1988.
14. Policy #270, ACLU.
15. The discussion benefits from a paper by William Curran, Larry Gostin, and Mary Clark, "Acquired Immunodeficiency Syndrome: Legal and Regulatory Policy," published by the Harvard School of Public Health, 1986. Their criteria include (1) "true purpose" (public health vs. disguised prejudice); (2) scientific evidence of a "public health necessity"; (3) the measures themselves cannot be a source of illness; and (4) the measures must be related to the public health goal.

    Also, James F. Childress, "An Ethical Framework for Assessing Policies to Screen for Antibodies to HIV," *Aids and Public Policy Journal* 2(Winter 1987):28–32. He suggests four conditions that will allow "infringing" on established rules: (1) the infringing policy must be effective; (2) no alternatives must be available; (3) one must seek the least infringing rules; and (4) one must disclose the policy to those being infringed upon.

    Finally see James F. Childress, "Contact Tracing: A Liberal Communitarian Approach," *The Responsive Community* 1 (Winter 1990–91): 69–77.
16. Gary S. Becker, "The Hot Air Inflating the Greenhouse Effect," *Business Week*, June 17, 1991, 16; Peter Passell, "Curing the Greenhouse Effect Could Run into the Trillions," *The New York Times*, November 19, 1989.
17. Mark Granzotto, "No: Random Roadblocks Are Ineffective," *ABA Journal* (April 1990): 45.
18. Paul M. Barrett and Amy Stevens, "Corporate Sentencing Plan Faces Hurdles," *The Wall Street Journal*, April 29, 1991, B4.
19. Ibid.
20. Paul Glastris, ". . . One That Should Be the Best, *But Isn't*," *The Washington Monthly*, March 1988, 31.
21. Ibid.
22. Peter Besinger, *USA Today*, February 17, 1988, 8A.
23. Galstris, "One That Should Be the Best," 31–32.
24. *The New York Times*, August 30, 1991.
25. Ibid.
26. Robert E. Goodin, "The Ethics of Smoking," *Ethics* 99 (April 1989):575.
27. Ibid., 574.
28. Ibid., 574–624.
29. Willard G. Manning, Emmett B. Keeler, Joseph P. Newhouse, Elizabeth M. Sloss, and Jeffrey Wasserman, "The Taxes of Sin: Do Smokers and Drinkers Pay Their Way?" *Journal of the American Medical Association* 26 (March 17, 1989):1607.
30. Goodin, "The Ethics of Smoking," 585.
31. George F. Will, "Smoking, Custom and the Law," *The Washington Post*, January 14, 1990, B7.
32. Ibid.
33. Stephen Wermiel, "Miranda Ruling Continues to Fall Under Attack; Some Critics See It as Law Enforcement Barrier," *The Wall Street Journal*, September 8, 1987.

34. "Respecting the Vitality of *Miranda*": The Case for Preserving the Right to Remain Silent" (Washington, DC: ACLU Foundation, 1988), 1.
35. Elder Witt, "Decision Trims Miranda Rule on Statements," *Congressional Quarterly* (March 9, 1985): 455.
36. Elder Witt, "High Court Holds the Line on *Miranda* Rule," *Congressional Quarterly* (January 31, 1987):196.
37. *Massachusetts v. Sheppard*, 468 U.S. 981-93 (1984).
38. "School Discipline: Recent Developments in Student Due Process Rights," *Michigan Bar Journal* (November 1989):1066.
39. See, generally, Emogene C. Wilhelm, "Note, Academic or Disciplinary Decisions: When Is Due Process Required: Campbell v. Board of Education," *Bridegeport Law Review* 6 (1985): 391-430; Albert S. Miles, "The Due Process of Students in Public School or College Disciplinary Hearings," *Alabama Lawyer*, 48 (May 1987):144-46. For an example of a state court modifying state policy see Jones v. Pascagoula Municipal School District, 524 So. 2d 968 (Mississippi, 1988).
40. "Elementary School Students' Civil Liberties," Policy #77, ACLU, 153a.
41. Amitai Etzioni, *The We Generation* (New York: Crown 1993).
42. Roger Conner, "The Checkpoint at Inkster: Reasonable or Unreasonable" *The Responsive Community* 1 (Winter 1990-91): 88-91.
43. Roger Conner, "Targeted Anti-Loitering Laws: Constitutional Violation or Community Protection" *The Responsive Community* 1 (Spring 1991):65-88.
44. Ibid., 66.
45. Stuart Taylor, Jr., "Trashing the Fourth Amendment, Again," *Manhattan Lawyer* (March 28, 1989):10.
46. "Mandatory Contact Tracing," a report of the AIDS and Civil Liberties Project, ACLU Foundation, 1-4.
47. Ibid., 2.
48. Ibid.
49. Jean Latz Griffin, "Rumors Raise Havoc with AIDS Testing Programs," *Chicago Tribune*, August 5, 1987.
50. "Mandatory Name Reporting," ACLU Foundation, 3.
51. "Mandatory Contact Tracing," ACLU Foundation, 2.
52. "Respecting the Validity of *Miranda*," ACLU Foundation, 3.
53. See, for example, Granzotto, "Random Roadblocks," 45.

4

Health-Care Rationing: A Critical Evaluation

"Too Much Care": A Value Judgment

Receiving increasing attention recently is the notion that Americans are obtaining "too much" health care and that if the government expects to control the growth in health-care expenditures, it will have to ration such services.[1] Also under discussion is the idea that we ought to foster a morality of self-imposed limitations on the care we seek.[2] Medical resources dedicated to "nonpersons" who are alive, such as the 10,000 patients kept in a vegetative state, or use in procedures that are futile and inhumane, are *not* at issue. Rather, the question is whether to curtail resources now provided to people with the capacity to recover, such as bone marrow transplants, kidney dialysis, and total parenteral nutrition.

These are far from merely theoretical discussions: In 1988 the state of Oregon announced that it would no longer pay for bone marrow transplants for its Medicaid patients, and similar statewide rationing schemes are being discussed in Arizona, Alaska, Colorado, Kentucky, and Vermont.[3] Countries such as Great Britain, which provides kidney dialysis for about one-third the number of patients who are served in the United States, are in effect engaging in such rationing. The most explicit rationing system yet is the Oregon Health Services Commission's announcement in 1990 to begin limiting even more health services according to a computer-ranked list of 1,600 medical procedures. The Oregon legislature will later vote on where to draw the line on this list, compiled by a formula balancing costs and expected benefits, with the understanding that all procedures falling below that line will not be reimbursed by Medicaid.

Rationing is defined as "the denial of commodities to those who have the money to buy them." In this sense, sugar, gasoline, and meat were rationed during World War II. The question now being raised is whether

51

health care should be rationed in the same way, whether its availability should be limited even to those who can pay for it.[4] *Rationing*, as the term is used in this chapter, is not to be confused with the other form of allocation of assets that is also sometimes referred to as "rationing" by the market. There, the depth of one's pockets rather than some social definition of one's worth, determines the amount of health one is able to purchase.

Most advocates of rationing recognize that to decide how much of a country's resources are to be dedicated to health care is to make a value judgment. Aaron and Schwartz put it as follows:

> Every nation must decide how much to spend on medical care and which services to buy. The decision on how much to spend expresses a judgement about the value of medical services relative to that of other consumption and investment. Whether Britain or the United States spends more or less than it "should" is an issue that we are unqualified to resolve.[5]

However, many who favor rationing health care then add some factual statements that seem to justify "objectively" the need to ration. For example, they state that health costs have risen more rapidly than has the overall rate of inflation, but neglect to mention that this is typical of all services compared to the price of commodities; hence the trend does not indicate any particular problem in this sector. Or they point out that the United States spends more of its gross national product on health care than do other nations. But this is due, at least in part, to the fact that the United States is richer than other nations.[6] The observation that Americans pay more for the same services than, say, do the British (i.e., that Americans get less health care per dollar spent) is not, per se, an indication that we are spending "too much" on health care, but shows only that we produce health care inefficiently.

Fuchs argues that the increase in health-care expenditures "has a particularly traumatic effect on other sectors."[7] This is far from self-evident. If a shortage of funds exists in some sector, say, housing for the homeless, it cannot be blamed on any other specific sector. Indeed, the shortage might as likely have been caused by the defense sector, the rising interest we pay on the national deficit, or that we have not found ways to increase the growth rate of the economy.

The most commonly repeated statement is that the proportion of the GNP spent on health care in the United States rose from 9.1 percent in 1980 to 10.9 percent in 1986 and is expected to rise to 15 percent by the year 2000. It is often implied, if not stated outright, that this rise indicates a "crisis".[8] Typically, however, no reasons are typically provided to indicate why any particular percentage should be viewed as the "proper" level of health-care expenditure (say, 9 percent), while some other figure (e.g., 15 percent) is, on the face of it, excessive. In short, arguments that the United States is spending "too much" on health care are based in part on value judgments, and need to be evaluated accordingly. This chapter critically examines the ethical reasons advanced both for rationing health care and for supporting an ethics of self-denial.

One's evaluation of rationing, as we shall see, is different according to whose funds are being used. However, whether the funds come from private, insured, or public funds, none of the arguments seems to justify rationing (section A). In particular, it seems unethical and erroneous to argue that some health measures (say, kidney dialysis) ought to be curtailed in order to "leave" funds for others (e.g., prenatal care) without examining *non*health sources that could be cut (e.g., obsolete military bases or waste and profiteering within the health sector; see section B). Particularly questionable is the notion that one ought to cut "excessive" acute care to gain funds for more preventive care (section C). The suggestion that life extension often buys years of poor quality existence is critically assessed (section D). It is further noted that the ethic of self-denial has some rather troubling side effects (section E). The chapter closes with an exploration of the ill consequences of the suggested measures for social justice (section F).

A. Private, Insured, or Public Funds

The argument that society should interfere in people's decisions to purchase more health services has to be assessed according to which resources people are using to make these purchases: their own funds, insurance pools, or taxpayers' monies. As long as people use their own dollars, our society abides by the code of "consumer sovereignty," which dictates that we should not, as a society, seek to influence their choices unless there is a compelling social need. Thus far, we allow people to buy basically anything they wish to buy, even if their choices are useless, tasteless, or unhealthy (e.g., cigarettes and alcohol). We ban only a few select items commonly labeled "drugs" or "controlled substances." Americans are free to spend their dollars on cosmetics, acquire new-model cars, keep their lawns green, and so on. What is the ethical rationale for prohibiting them from reslicing *their* pie if they wish to buy fewer of these items and more health services—even if some of them are only marginally beneficial or of dubious value? To put it more precisely: Is there a reason to add, in effect, some items of health care, say, hip replacements for those over eighty, to the list of controlled substances?

It might be argued that if Americans continue to increase their spending on health services, soon they will be "short" all other things. But if and when this becomes the case, *they* will feel the pinch and *they* will be free to rearrange their mix of purchases in some other way, say, by buying less cosmetic surgery (a health-care item) and more designer jeans (an "allowed" consumer good).

Several economists have argued that Americans buy more health care than they would buy if they had to pay for it directly, because they use "third party" dollars through various insurance plans. This alleged propensity is often "demonstrated" by the following tale:

> The most fundamental point is captured by the close analogy between the way we pay for health-care and the pooled restaurant check. If you and I and a large number of other people go to dinner (a group similar in size to the typical health group, for example) and if we agree in advance to share the check evenly among each diner, there is a powerful incentive for each person to order more costly food than he or she would when dining alone and paying the full cost.[9]

True, these purchases drive up the price paid for health insurance, that is, premiums. To the extent that those insured pay premiums directly, there seems, again, no reason within our kind of system to interfere— even if this leads to some "distortions" in what people buy. After all, economists do not argue against other insurance schemes, such as life insurance policies, in which consumers' "bad" judgments are much more evident. Very few consumers purchasing life insurance understand what they buy; obviously their knowledge about what they will get, payable only after death, is much weaker than their knowledge of health insurance. Most experts believe people should buy term insurance and not "life," but they buy more "life" because that is the one sellers profit from more and push harder.

Turning now to most insurance plans that are paid for in full or in part by employers, the proper control mechanism for these is already in place. When employers judge that the costs of premiums are too high, they either provide less costly, more limiting insurance, or negotiate with their employees to choose between more meager health benefits but increases in other areas (e.g., salary), or vice versa. Indeed, in several instances, workers clearly indicated that they would rather keep greater health benefits and give up some other items. Pittston Corporation mineworkers, for example, settled a long strike by granting the corporation greater latitude in reassigning workers and keeping the mines open seven days a week in exchange for maintaining their completely employer-provided health coverage, instead of reducing the percentage to 80 percent, which was favored by Pittston.[10] In other cases, the opposite result has been negotiated; however, health care is almost always included in the bargaining.[11]

What reason exists for society to interfere in the *mix* of compensation employers provide their employees? One may argue that compensation is too high for the United States to be competitive, or too high for men and too low for women, referring to the *total* package (i.e., wages and all benefits). But there is much less of an issue over how the package is internally composed, that is, whether 70 percent goes to wages and 30 percent to health care, or 68 percent to 32 percent, or some other such mix.

Turning now to the use of tax revenues, there is no reliable, objective, or scientific guide to determine the "right" way to distribute tax dollars among defense, education, welfare, health, and other major segments of public expenditures. Statements pressing us to spend more on welfare, foreign aid, or some other need reflect differences among social philosophies and personal values. Since as a society we cannot come to any detailed consensus on these matters, we use the political process (elections, the legislature, courts, and so on) to work out an agreed pattern of allocation. For nearly twenty-five years now, the consensus has been to allocate a growing proportion of our tax revenues to health expenditures.

Is this policy out of step with the freely and properly expressed wishes of American voters? Far from it. A June 1988 poll showed that 67 percent of Americans favor increasing government spending on health care compared with a mere 26 percent who were in favor of more spending on space programs. Thirty-five percent would like to spend less on the military and defense, but only 3 percent is in favor of reducing government spending on health care.[12] Another poll found that between 1984 and 1986, on average, almost two-thirds of Americans believed that the nation was not spending enough on improving and protecting the nation's health; only 7 percent thought we were spending too much.[13] Other polls show similar results. *When voters, elected representatives, and public policies proceed hand in hand, no one should step in to try to pull them asunder unless there is a rather compelling reason.* As the rest of this analysis argues, no such reason seems in evidence.

B. Subsystem versus System Rationing

Is American society so hard-pressed that it should consider rationing health care or asking its infirm and elderly to, in effect, put themselves out on the ice and quietly freeze to death (as Eskimos are said to do) in order to stop soaking up more health services?[14] If ration we must, it seems unethical to ration resources used to sustain life, without *first* considering curtailing other expenditures of much less merit. Examples abound, but we might start by cutting back on some of the recent, large increases in the budget for exploration of Mars and other space visitations: $15.1 billion for fiscal year 1991 (FY 1991).[15] Better yet, what about eliminating the *$30 billion* military stockpile of obsolete tools and rotting uniforms, such as 150,000 pairs of Korean War vintage cold-weather pants, that are filling up armed forces warehouses to the point that newer, needed items (e.g., parts for helicopters) are being left outside to be damaged or destroyed by the elements?[16] Or why not cut obsolete federal subsidy programs, such as one dating back to 1949 that pays a relatively small group of beekeepers subsidies of $184 million annually (beekeepers' production of wax was encouraged by the use of public funds in World War II to meet the needs of our troops' wet boots)?[17]

To put it in more technical terms, if we are to rationalize the distribution of resources, why *sub*optimize, by only "straightening out" our health-care budget? Why not rationalize the whole government budget, and look for nonhealth items that could be curtailed with much less sacrifice of people's needs and preferences? It must be noted that in our present political system, any ideas to allocate resources with even a semblance of rationality systemwide or subsystemwide are merely wishful thinking. Congress is so dominated by special interests that allocations are driven to a very large extent by who pays more for the enormous costs of reelection than by any other criteria. One constructive policy idea after another is perverted by these pressures.

It follows that any concern with efficient allocation of resources among societal needs, not to mention across-the-board or even sectorial rationalizations, requires first and foremost a major movement of political reform. *Much more would be achieved for the economy if instead of rationing health care or anything else, we would (1) ban private financial contributions to congressional campaigns,* as we did for presidential elections; (2) extend the terms of members of the House to four years; (3) limit campaign periods; and (4) make a few other such changes widely endorsed by public interest groups and experts.

It should be acknowledged that even if this were achieved, we still would not have, nor should we seek, the central planning in effect advocated by some of the champions of rationing. Such planning is a logical outgrowth of trying to ensure that every public dollar will be spent where it will bring the largest marginal utility. When we replace individual choice with guidelines, someone has to decide what is in and what is out. Indeed, Callahan[18] explicitly calls for a federal government agency to determine what our societal health needs are and to allot funds and limit care, nationwide, according to these needs. But experience—not just in the USSR, but during Prohibition, in the war against drugs, and with guidelines already introduced into health care—teaches us that this approach is extremely inefficient, alienating, and ultimately unworkable.

If and when there is a clear and present unmet public need, limited and indirect context-setting interventions work best. For instance, one may reduce the number of new hospital beds that can be reimbursed rather than centrally determine the use of each bed. Better yet, cap the annual growth rate of health funds available per region, adjusted to changes in population size, age, and other attributes, rather than ration specific services. Far from being a radical idea, this is already being done, and more such plans are being recommended.[19] Meanwhile, as long as the health-care "crisis" does not pinch much more that it does, matters as sacred as life and as personal as health care are best left subject to individual give-and-take among patients, their families, and health-care professionals.

Finally, if for some reason, which I cannot discern, the savings must come from health expenditures, surely we must first reduce the estimated 22 percent of our health-care dollars spent on billing and other administrative tasks. Compared to a doubling in the number of doctors between 1970 and 1986, the number of health administrators quadrupled.[20] Or why not begin by reducing the 33.5 cents per dollar spent by private health insurers on administrative tasks in 1988?[21]

We could also proceed by cutting the billions spent on *unnecessary* medical procedures,[22] such as many cesareans and cataract operations.[23] The former secretary of health, education, and welfare, Joseph Califano, among other health-care professionals, estimates that between 25 percent and 50 percent of health services and operations performed in this country are unnecessary.[24] Dr. Robert Brook of the RAND Corporation reports that 25 percent of all days that patients spend in the hospital are unnecessary, as, for example, a patient who spent an additional night in the hospital only because she needed to take oral medication twice the following day.[25]

And before we ration services, we should find ways to curb defensive medicine—say, by limiting the amount lawyers can collect in malpractice suits or by limiting unnecessary procedures ordered by doctors anxious to protect themselves from lawsuits. A man complaining of a stomach pain after eating a big dinner, for example, may come into an emergency room and be tested in general ways to determine whether he has coronary artery disease. The test is not fully accurate, so those with heart disease may be misled and assured of their good health. Occasionally, taking the test causes complications from which patients may die; and those who are incorrectly labeled ill will also suffer. But the test may nevertheless be ordered because the patient has a *5 percent chance* of having coronary artery disease.[26]

Finally, before rationing services, we should limit the extent to which we maintain 10,000 people in persistent vegetative states who have no human function or future.[27]

It is argued that *these* cuts would lead to one-time savings, but that rationing would lead to continued savings. While this is true for at least some of these cuts, it is morally unacceptable to cut life-extending items before tackling those expenditures with no such implications (e.g., reducing paperwork before eliminating liver transplants for children).

C. The Social Work Hand-Off

Different authorities on the subject have their own ideas of what they would cut first once they achieved health-care rationing. One recommendation, however, has gained a wider following and deserves special examination. This is the suggestion that we spend too much on high-tech acute care and not enough on preventive measures, "which are of comparable or greater importance, even if less glamorous or profitable".[28] As a typical example, cases such as the following are often cited: A homeless person lives on a street near the George Washington Hospital. Occasionally, especially when the weather is cold, he is brought to the emergency room, tested in a variety of ways, and often ends up in the intensive care unit. After rehabilitation, he is returned to the street. The cost of his hospital care is immense and is said to be irrational. It would be much more efficient to provide him with decent housing or even welfare, thus *preventing* a good number of his illnesses and saving on the use of high-tech acute care. More generally, it is often argued that it is much more efficient to provide drug education than to deal with crack babies; to prevent teen pregnancies than to deal with underweight, premature, and malnourished infants; to regulate guns than to cope with the victims of violence, and so on.

When one examines these claims critically, initially their inner logic seems unquestionably true. Prevention is much more economical and humane than *post hoc* treatment. It should be noted, however, that very often the lack of available funds is only part of the problem; hence, the idea that we would be better off if we transferred funds from acute to preventive care is not necessarily so in many situations.

Starting with the case at hand, many of the homeless are mental patients. Courts have determined that they have a right to refuse to move into public shelters, which many of them do. To provide preventive care in this case would require violating their rights, or changing our basic concepts as to what these are. Similarly, drugs, teen pregnancy, and violence are the results of *several* highly complex sociological, psychological, and political forces.[29] As a consequence, attempts by educated people to follow a healthier way of life are rather limited in their success. Take, for example, the effort to educate people about the risk of AIDS. In New York City, from 1976 to 1984 the percentage that engaged in anal intercourse had dropped from 80 percent to 46 percent. But a study in San Francisco showed that in 1985, almost three years after the launching of educational campaigns, 25 percent of the men were still engaging in high-risk sexual contact at least once a month, though fully 90 percent of them knew it to be dangerous. And many who engaged in safe sex for a while returned to unsafe practices.

The impact of AIDS education was even poorer in areas less afflicted with the AIDS virus. In cities such as Pittsburgh, 65 percent of the men in one study were still engaging in anal intercourse. Again, 90 percent of them knew they ought to wear condoms, yet 62 percent of them said they rarely or never used them.[30] Educational campaigns to educate women about the danger of taking Acutane, a powerful acne medicine that causes birth defects, have failed.[31]

Nor can these deep-seated social problems be corrected by reallocation of funds. Coping with them is best not perceived at all as part of preventive health care, but as part of general societal restructuring and moral recommitment. Thus, for example, while it is true that emergency rooms in many cities are overloaded with victims of gunshot wounds, that does not mean that one can take on gun control as part of health care; otherwise, the whole world's defects would be encompassed in preventive health care. The health-care system must, unfortunately, take these social problems, by and large, as given. It is certainly worthwhile to keep calling attention to them, but to suggest that they could be significantly fixed as part of a rationalization of health care is unreasonable.

D. Junk Health?

Aside from arguing that we are purchasing "too much" health, and health of the "wrong" kind, we are also told that we are obtaining worthless items. We are said to be driven by an irrational quest for immortality or silver bullets that will kill off all disease and that we are, in effect, paying ever more for meaningless services, for "health care" that extends life without any consideration of its quality.

In evaluating this claim, a distinction must be made between extending lives of *no* discernible quality, and those some select observers (but not the patients) judge to be of *insufficient* quality. The first kind is found in patients for whom there is no consciousness, no ability to function as a human being, to work, create, care for others, or sense that one is being cared for. A case in point are the more than 10,000 Americans considered to be in a persistent vegetative state, many of whom are maintained in nursing homes.[32] Here, there is no quality of life, in effect no *human* life, and next to no prospect that it might be resumed. Hence, there seems to be some moral justification in discontinuing health services to these "nonpersons." There also seems to be a case for curtailing the much more common, and costly, surgical and other medical procedures performed on people at the very end of their lives, when there is no discernible value to these measures. In these cases, the patients should be placed in hospices to ameliorate pain and extend care rather than be subject to extensive surgical or other medical intervention. And certainly, procedures that committees of physicians judge to be both "futile and inhumane"[33]—such as those used to keep alive a two-year-old infant who had spent its life in and out of the hospital, had undergone various surgical procedures, and ended up being kept alive on ventilators, able neurologically to experience only pain[34]—should not be provided.

Yet termination of such services is opposed on the ground that it might push us down a slippery slope, whereby once we terminate service to some, we shall soon terminate it to old but functioning people, to the disabled, to minorities, and so on. Typical of this thinking is Callahan's fear of the "corruption" of euthanasia (behind which lie references to the belief that "some lives are not worth living"), which, he says, "may well have contributed a poisonous background condition that made the Nazi atrocities more likely."[35]

To guard against such slippage, we must draw clear lines of demarcation. For instance, we would "pull the plug" only on those patients who pass the judgment of two physicians analyzing the situation according to some clear lines—or lines that can be legitimated (e.g., by a living will) and expressed in laws and procedures, as in hospital review committees. To prevent slippage also requires public education to introduce new concepts of dying and to nurture acceptance of pulling the plug under carefully designated conditions, rather than routinely "doing all one can for a loved one." Much of this education is already taking place, and more can be initiated. (Whether or not the treatment of, extremely premature infants, for example, falls into this category requires a detailed review that cannot be undertaken here.) Whatever position one takes on these matters, it is an odd position indeed to argue that it is morally appropriate to terminate services to living people who seek kidney dialysis, but not appropriate to cut off costly life-support systems extending the lives of people in persistent vegetative states because such acts may lead, down the road, to terminating services to people of higher capacity. It is like saying we should not have fire extinguishers in the home because it may prompt children to play with matches.

The situation is radically different for procedures that are dedicated to extending conscious, caring, creative, and often productive life, even when they impose some travail and constraints. A procedure often cited as a candidate for elimination is kidney dialysis.[36] Some patients choose not to have it; most, however prefer being fettered to a machine three times a week for four hours or so and suffering attendant side effects such as itchy skin, depression, and fatigue to dying. What is ethically unacceptable about that decision? That it is economically not troubling we have already seen. Indeed, it would be highly troubling to refuse services to people who can recover to a significant extent, say, to 85 percent capacity. The denial of treatment to kidney dialysis patients seems even more questionable when one considers the effects of a new drug, Recombinant Erythropoietin (EPO), which has significantly improved the quality of life of dialysis patients according to both objective standards (patients experienced fewer symptoms of anemia, had less of a need for transfusions, had fewer infections associated with transfusions, and were more physically active) and subjective criteria (patients reported increased well-being and life satisfaction).[37]

If we refuse treatments such as kidney dialysis and hip replacements, what shall we refuse next? While there is a clear line of demarcation between serving those who are only biologically alive but not humanly, there is no such line between kidney dialysis, and, say, hip replacements and many other clearly beneficial procedures. If we are to curtail these services, to what morally more compelling purposes are we to dedicate these "saved" resources?

E. Side Effects of "Enough Is Enough"

Beyond rationing by force, some ethicists, especially Callahan,[38] have called for self-imposed limitations on how much health care we consume. He argues that it is morally inappropriate to soak up ever more resources in a vain pursuit of ever more years.

> I have before my mind's eye a future healthcare system that seeks not to constantly conquer all disease and extend all life, but which seeks instead to enhance the quality of life; which seeks not always to overcome the failings and decline of the body, but helps people better cope with them . . . which works to help society curb its appetite for ever higher quality and constant improvements in healthcare. . . . We are bounded and finite beings, ineluctably subject to aging, decline, and death.[39]

This ethic of "enough is enough," a kind of latter-day counter culture idea (less is more; small is beautiful; achievement and success, science and technology are suspect), mixed with traditional Catholic notions of acquiescence (we should accept our fate in this world rather than fight it), has serious deleterious consequences. It does not take into account the fact that health care often entails considerable efforts by members of the family, nurses, and physicians. Hence, an ethic that justifies fewer efforts would make it more acceptable for family members to dump the infirm in public institutions, and might well, whether it is foreseen or not, further encourage nursing home owners to skimp on everything from nursing to antibiotics.

Some evidence to this effect is found in a study in Britain in which doctors report that they routinely talk patients out of procedures they, the physicians, consider costly. As one doctor there put it:

> The sense that I have is that there are many situations where resources are sufficiently short so that there must be decisions made as to who is treated. Given that circumstance, the physician, in order to live with himself and to sleep well at night, has to look at the arguments for not treating a patient. And there are always some—social, medical, whatever. In many instances he heightens, sharpens, or brings into focus the negative component in order to make himself and the patient more comfortable about not going forward.[40]

Similarly, in Sweden "doctors tend to withhold treatment from the beginning from infants for whom statistical data suggest a grim prognosis."[41] I am not sure on what ethical grounds this practice is legitimated. In any event, in Britain, doctors are salaried and hence have less conflict of interest than they do in the United States.

If the same curtailing approach were used here, doctors would be much more likely to talk down procedures that generate less profit, while recommending those that have a high return rate. For example, doctors who own their own X-ray machines are reported to order 40 percent to 60 percent more Xrays than others for the same mix of patients; a 1983 Blue Cross and Blue Shield study found that laboratories owned by referring physicians performed nearly twice as many tests and charged almost twice as much to the average patient.[42] Another study of a for-profit medical clinic that introduced a new bonus program that gauged physicians' earnings according to their charges per patient found that doctors there ordered 23 percent more lab tests per appointment and 16 percent more xrays during a three month period.[43] This is hardly a world one could ethically favor, nor is it economically more efficient than the one it seeks to replace.

F. Three Matters of Equity

Economists have sensitized us to the important observation that changes in the total number of resources available (due to slower economic growth, recession, inflation, or simple budgetary changes—or rationing) will tend to affect different subpopulations differently. In plain English, when the amounts of feed available change, some oxen starve, some get gored, and some feed more lavishly. The question of which social groups are particularly likely to be hurt or to benefit from health rationing and self-limitation must be systematically included in any evaluation of the suggested measures. Here, this question is examined from three viewpoints: intergenerational equity, consumers versus providers, and the well-off versus the poor and the near-poor.

The Old, the Young, and Nonintrinsic Criteria

Callahan explicitly calls for stopping all but ameliorative care (pain killers, nursing, and emotional support), especially for those in their late seventies or early eighties, but also for some other groups.[44] Britain, in effect, follows his recommendation for many of its elderly. For those over the age of sixty-five, dialysis was provided to only about one-tenth the number of patients treated in other advanced countries.[45] Between 1964 and 1984 in Britain the average wait for a hip replacement was eighteen months and often as long as five years.[46] Like all allocations, bans, or prohibitions based on a nonrelevant criterion—whether it is race, religion, gender, or age—rationing health care to the elderly is clearly discriminatory. By nonrelevant criteria we mean those based on attributes not directly health-related, such as age rather than capacity to benefit from the use of resources.

The point can be readily illustrated by comparing two cases. Imagine one person who is eighty-two, a creative writer and loving spouse, who is taking care of a husband suffering from Alzheimer's disease and who supports her grandchildren. She has a disease that can be readily treated and from which she can recover to full functioning, but which, if not treated, is life-threatening (for example, pneumonia). The other person is thirty-six, a convicted criminal and asocial, who has terminal cancer. What is the moral justification for providing acute care to the second but not to the first?

To further highlight the point, assume both have the same sociological attributes (make them both creative, loving, etc.), but the older one can be restored to full life and the younger one is definitely terminal and in a late stage of deterioration. Clearly, ameliorative care should be assigned to the younger, and acute to the older. That is, if health care is to be rationed, in order for that rationing to be nondiscriminatory, it should be allotted according to the ability to benefit from the resources as determined by medical criteria, not mechanically according to age or some other such nonrelevant criteria.

Consumers versus Providers

A surprisingly large proportion of the discussion of health-care costs focuses on the "consumers", and much less attention is paid to the role played by providers. For instance, it is repeatedly stressed that consumers "buy" inordinately high amounts of health care because they do not use their own money but are reimbursed by third-party dollars. However, the image of a market driven by consumers, in which providers must keep their profits down in order to stay competitive, is at best partially applicable to health care. It is well established that most of the decisions about which health-care resources to consume are not made by the consumers but by the providers. Once a patient presents herself or himself, physicians and institutions make most of the decisions about which procedures to order, the length of stay in the hospital, and so on

For this reason, if one wishes to curb costs, the *providers* are the best place to focus one's attention. What should physicians' fees be? Should they be allowed to have other profitable interests in the care of their own patients? And what should the role of profit-making corporations be in health care? In the past five years, doctors' salaries have risen 30 percent, compared to an average 16.3 percent increase in wages and salaries for all other full-time workers.[47] In 1988 the average physician in America was making $144,700 per year; one-fourth of them were making more than $180,000,[48] putting physicians in the top 3 percent on the American income scale.[49] Indeed, American physicians earn much more than their counterparts in other countries, many living royal lifestyles unheard-of in other countries.

American physicians themselves often state that they are being paid too much. One doctor noted, "It's always nice to be overcompensated for your work. And I think you can argue that I have been."[50] American physicians are paid by service rather than by salary, and they have growing proprietary interests in laboratories, technologies, and even in the drugs their patients consume.[51] Many are organized like profit-making corporations. For example, the chief of service in pathology or anesthesiology contracts to provide a hospital with a service and hence benefits the less he or she spends. The result is often less-qualified staff, such as anesthesiologists who cannot communicate with the surgical team because they have a poor command of English. Also, the proportion of health care provided by profit-making corporations has increased, whereas in the previous decade much more was provided by so-called private, but actually voluntary, not-for-profit hospitals and nursing homes.

Addressing the question of whether these arrangements are efficient or morally appropriate would require a sizable book, if not several volumes. (Actually, several have already been written.)[52] The most we can note here is that any proposal that seeks to curtail services available to patients but does not also examine ways to curtail physicians' profits as a way to reduce costs is ethically incomplete, if not biased. In the never-never land of perfect competition, the difference in focus has no significance, because if the consumers all flock to the source of the best product at the lowest cost, physicians whose profits are excessive will have no patients. However, in a world of monopolistic behavior and products that "consumers" buy with little understanding, other rules prevail. Limiting the excessive profits that physicians enjoy, for example, by ordering unnecessary tests and procedures, is a question that must be addressed before one argues for, say, curtailing bone marrow transplants. Ration profits before lives.

Effects on the Poor and Near-Poor

Because it can be used to override market forces (which allocate resources to people according to their wealth and income), rationing is often introduced to enhance fairness or social justice and to ensure that all consumers will have access to select products deemed essential. Thus, when gasoline is in short supply, rather than allocating it by higher prices—which, in effect, means that the rich will be able to buy all the gasoline they wish while the poor will walk—providing each individual with X gallons (more for those who need cars for their work) enhances social justice. It should be stressed, however, that health-care rationing as commonly discussed is of a radically different sort. It denies the poor and near-poor, penalizes the middle classes, and as a rule, does not curb the rich, for the basic reason that health-care rationing generally takes place through refusals to reimburse for certain treatments, rather than through rationing of the actual service. Thus, when the state of Oregon decided to ration bone marrow transplants, it cut reimbursements for those on Medicaid. That is, those who could pay the $100,000 bill out of their own pockets could have it (as could those who could afford to move to neighboring California). In New Hampshire in the early 1980s, when Medicaid recipients were restricted to three prescriptions per month, it was the poor who suffered, particularly the elderly, who tend to suffer from illnesses such as diabetes, asthma, and heart disease that require multiple pills to treat them.[53] Similarly, as Schwartz noted,

> "Britain is not egalitarian in the sense that everyone gets the same kind of care. A private health-care system has developed which allows people with means to circumvent the three-or four-year queue for a hip replacement and the long delays for other types of elective surgery."[54]

As a result, about one-fourth of all hip replacements in Britain and Wales are paid for privately,[55] while the other three-fourths wait in line.

Some argue that it is proper to proceed by rationing, although it will largely disadvantage the poor and near-poor (the well-off will be able to buy most services on the side) because the poor are already disadvantaged - they ride in buses and not cars, and live in smaller houses than the rich. The said approach merely extends the prevailing class structure to health care. In effect, of course, they are already in place in health care, but the suggestion is to extend their reach. It is indeed true that there is such a societal pattern, common in many societies, although more pronounced in the United States than in most other Western democracies. And it should be noted that by several criteria, during the 1980's the poor declined, while the rich grew richer. The question is whether at this juncture we should seek to extend their misery, especially in matters of health, or whether, if we must cut health care, we should look for approaches that would not impose extra burdens on the most vulnerable members of our society.

Conclusion

Many of the arguments in favor of health-care rationing are based on implicit assumptions that we can have a society in which our resources are allocated according to some economist's notion of efficiency, in which the "marginal" dollars are spent where they bring the greatest benefit. In a society dominated by special-interest groups, profiteering, and monopolistic behavior within the professions—and with a growing role for profit-making corporations in the health-care area— rationing will have very different consequences: it will tend to hurt the poor and the elderly, but not necessarily benefit the health care of any other group; waste and abuse will continue unabashedly in this and other sectors. Because there are places where a reduction in services would not endanger lives, services in these sectors should be on the cutting block before rationing health care is considered—that is, if we *are* so hard-pressed that rationing of any kind is in order.

If and when it comes to rationing within the health-care sector, we need to be sure that services that have no discernible medical merit (such as those that may be deemed "futile and inhumane" and those provided to patients unable to regain functioning) are curtailed before services for people clearly able to regain their health are rationed, and before such services as kidney dialysis, which some ethicists (but not the patients themselves) deem to be of insufficient quality, are limited.

Notes

1. Henry J. Aaron and William B. Schwartz, *The Painful Prescription* (Washington, DC: The Brookings Institution, 1984); Aaron and Schwartz, "Rationing Health Care: The Choice Before Us," *Science* 247, (1990): 418–22; American Medical Association, "Memorandum re: Resolution 66 (A–87)," October 1987; Michael D. Bayles, "Allocation of Scarce Medical Resources," *Public Affairs Quarterly* 4 (1990): 1–16; "Insider Interview, John D. Golenski, President, Bioethics Consultation Group," *HealthWeek*, July 17, 1989, 26, 29; David Mechanic, "Social Policy, Technology, and the Rationing of Health Care," *Medical Care Review* 46 (1989): 113–120; Daniel Wikler, "Persuasion and Coercion for Health: Ethical Issues in Government Efforts to Change Lifestyles," in *Contemporary Issues in Bioethics,* 2d ed., Tom L. Beauchamp and LeRoy Walters, eds. (Belmont, CA: Wadsworth, 1982).

2. Daniel Callahan, *What Kind of Life* (New York: Simon Schuster, 1990).
3. "Medicaid Rationing Plan Gaining Favor in Other States," *American Medical News* 32 (1989): 1.
4. Aaron and Schwartz, "Rationing Health Care," 418.
5. Aaron and Schwartz, *Painful Prescription*, 79.
6. Ibid,.
7. Victor R. Fuchs, "The Health Sector's Share of the Gross National Product," *Science* 247 (1990): 533-7.
8. *The Washington Post*, March 22, 1990, A22; *The Washington Post*, November 30, 1988, A23.
9. Private correspondence, March 1, 1990; see also Aaron and Schwartz, *Painful Prescription*, 7; Fuchs, "Health Sector's Share," 537; *The New York Times*, March 5, 1990, A22, D6.
10. *The Wall Street Journal*, February 20, 1990, A3.
11. See "National Policy for Steel Agreement," Bethlehem Steel Corporation, May 3, 1989; "Health Care and Other Benefits," AT&T Operations Bargaining Report, 1989.
12. Gallup Poll, Survey GO88149, Q5B, July 1988.
13. *Public Opinion* 10 (1987): 28.
14. Callahan, What kind of Life?, 1990.
15. *The New York Times*, February 2, 1990.
16. *The New York Times*, February 4, 1990.
17. *The Washington Post*, August 2, 1990, A29.
18. Callahan, What kind of Life, 199.
19. *New England Journal of Medicine* (February 15, 1990): 466.
20. *The New York Times*, February 19, 1990, A13.
21. *The Washington Post*, October 10, 1990, A21.
22. Aaron and Schwartz, "Rationing Health Care," 419.
23. *The Washington Post*, November 30, 1988, A23.
24. Robert H. Brook and Kathleen N. Lohr, "Will We Need to Ration Effective Health Care?" *Issues in Science and Technology* 3 (1986): 72, 73; *The Washington Post*, January 17, 1989, A24; *The Washington Post*, November 30, 1988, A23.
25. Brook and Lohr, "Will We Need to Ration Effective Health Care?," 72.
26. Ibid., 73.
27. *New England Journal of Medicine* 322 (1990): 1227.
28. Norman Daniels, *Just Health Care* (New York: Cambridge University Press, 1984), 14.
29. Ronald Bayer, *Private Acts, Social Consequences* (New York: The Free Press, 1989).
30. Bayer, Private Acts, 227-28.
31. *The Washington Post*, May 22, 1990, A9.
32. *The Washington Post*, November 25, 1989, A23.
33. *New England Journal of Medicine* 322 (1990):1013.
34. Ibid.
35. Callahan, What kind of Life?, 229.
36. Aaron and Schwartz, *Painful Prescription*, 29-37; Callahan, What Kind of Life?, 177; Daniel J. Koshland, Jr., Editorial, *Science* 247 (1990): 9.
37. Roger W. Evans et al., *"The Quality of Life of Hemodialysis Recipients Treated with Recombinant Human Erythropoietin,"* Journal of the American Medical Association 263 (1990): 825-30.

38. Callahan, What Kind of Life?.
39. Ibid., 22–23.
40. Aaron and Schwartz, "Rationing Health Care," 247.
41. Hastings Center Report cited in *The Washington Post*, March 18, 1990, B3.
42. *The Wall Street Journal*, March 1, 1989, A6.
43. *The Wall Street Journal*, April 12, 1990, B4.
44. Callahan, What Kind of Life?, 67.
45. "From Research to Rationing: A Conversation with William B. Schwartz," *Health Affairs* (Fall 1989):64.
46. *The New York Times*, May 30, 1990, A25.
47. Fuchs, Health Sector's Share, 535.
48. *The New York Times*, February 18, 1990.
49. *The Washington Post*, March 18, 1990, B3.
50. *The New York Times*, February 18, 1990.
51. *The New York Times Magazine*, November 5, 1989, 88+.
52. Rosemary Stevens, *In Sickness and in Wealth: American Hospitals in the Twentieth Century* (New York: Basic Books, 1989); Dan E. Beauchamp, *The Health of the Republic: Epidemics, Medicine, and Moralism as Challenges to Democracy* (Philadelphia: Temple University Press, 1988).
53. *The Wall Street Journal*, June 27, 1990, B1.
54. Schwartz, From Research to Rationing, 68.
55. Brook, and Lohr, "Will We Need to Ration Effective Health Care?" 70.

5

Voluntaristic Assumptions about Health Maintenance: Who Is in Charge Of Your Health?

A Hidden Ideological Bias

Few people realize that the Surgeon General's 1988 *Nutrition and Health* report is not altogether objective or scientific. While it draws on thousands of empirical studies, and involved 200 researchers, it strongly reflects a particular paradigm. Both its underlying thrust and its specific recommendations express a *laissez-faire*, conservative political philosophy and a closely related neoclassical social science paradigm. The central thesis of the report is that choices that *individuals freely* make significantly affect their life expectancy and their health.

> In recent years, scientific investigations have produced abundant information on the ways personal behavior affects health. This information can help us decide whether to smoke, when and how much to drink, how far to walk or climb stairs, whether to wear seat belts, and how or whether to engage in any other activity that might alter the risk of incurring disease or disability. For the two out of three adult Americans who do not smoke and do not drink excessively, one personal choice seems to influence long-term health prospects more than any other: what we eat.[1]

There are numerous other reports, articles, and books that contain the same viewpoint—for example, *Diet and Health* by the National Research Council. Their ideas and recommendations are carried prominently and repeatedly by the mass media (e.g., a cover story of *Newsweek* and a feature article in *The Boston Globe*). We use the examination of the report on *Nutrition and Health* to reflect on all of them.

A paradigm is most effective when its advocates and those subject to its appeals are unaware of a document's slant, and subsequently see the implied messages either as self-evident truth, or, better yet, as supported by science. (This is one reason that Marxists insist that their particular ideology derives from the *science* of history.) It is safe to assume that most, if not all, researchers and scholars involved in preparing the Surgeon General's report do not consider their work to be ideological. Most Americans are so imbued with the individualistic, *laissez-faire* paradigm that it is difficult to obtain a fair hearing when one attempts to discuss its implications. It is thus hardly surprising that the report's ideological bias, which deeply flaws its analysis and policies, went largely unobserved by authors and readers alike.

Critics of the report argue that it offers little new information. The notion that one's chosen "lifestyle" affects one's health far more than medical services has been gaining influence for more than two decades. Few, however, put the "responsibility" that individuals have for their health more clearly than Dr. John Knowles:

> Over 99 percent of us are born healthy and made sick as a result of personal misbehavior and environmental conditions. The solution to the problems of ill health in modern American society involves individual responsibility, in the first instance, and social responsibility through public legislative and private volunteer efforts, in the second instance.[2]

Knowles continues:

> Most individuals do not worry about their health until they lose it. . . . I believe the idea of a "right" to health (guaranteed by government) should be replaced by the idea of an individual moral obligation to preserve one's own health—a public duty, if you will.[3]

Joseph Califano, former secretary of the Department of Health, Education and Welfare (now Health and Human Services), gave even more credence to this view: "You, the individual, can do more for your own health and well-being than any doctor, any hospital, any drug, and any exotic medical device."[4] He also helps to perpetuate a magical longevity figure, citing a study that reports that those who "lived right" (observed certain health guidelines) "lived, on the average, eleven years longer than those who practiced none of them."[5]

The reason we can expect to hear more about the need to "live right" is that health costs are perceived to be rapidly rising, causing a crisis. Furthermore, a major cause for the increase, we are told, is the "irresponsibility" of the masses. "One critic, the physician and social philosopher Knowles (1977), was sufficiently disturbed by the fact that the larger society, rather than the individual, has to bear so much of the current costs of health care in the United States for the health conditions."[6]

Dr. C. Everett Koop's 1988 report on *Nutrition and Health* (from here on, simply "the report") legitimizes and officially sanctions this conclusion as only the Surgeon General can. Its position was further elaborated in 1989 in a 1,300-page report, *Diet and Health*, based on 5,000 studies, that was issued by the authoritative National Research Council.

The individualistically inclined public readily accepts the message. Sixty percent of Americans consider their health a personal responsibility.[7] Further, 92 percent of Americans agree that: "If we Americans ate more nutritious food, smoked less, maintained our proper weight, and exercised regularly, it would do more to improve our health than anything doctors and medicine can do for us."[8] Blech captures the prevailing mentality: "If I'm sick, it must be my fault. If my life is a mess, I've failed to fulfill my potential," and he concludes, "For every misfortune in life, we seem too ready to blame the victim."[9]

Alfred E. Harper, a professor of nutritional sciences at the University of Wisconsin,[10] points to the long tradition of attaching symbolic and mythical qualities to food. Myths, unlike science (he quotes Lévi-Strauss), give people only illusory, not actual, control over the environment. People now believe that they understand the nature of health and illness, and that eating "right" will significantly improve their condition.

Richard Evans, a psychologist, points out:

> It is becoming more fashionable to espouse a personal health (risk-factor reduction) ideology than ideologies related to racial and religious prejudice, the nuclear war threat, anti-environment pollution, and so on. . .
>
> We may be contributing to a type of mass hypochondriasis resulting in an increasingly diminishing freedom in human life-style and quality of life.[11]

Within days after the report's release, it became known that the second-largest convenience-food organization in the United States, Circle K, had decided to limit medical coverage to its employees based on "personal life-style decisions," such as AIDS, alcohol and drug abuse, and self-inflicted wounds.[12] Several corporations pay more to employees who improve their health in line with the stated philosophies.[13] Three percent of America's 500 largest corporations now offer plans that tie financial incentives to good health practices. Nine percent more plan to do so by 1993, and 19 percent are considering such a policy.[14] For example, T. Boone Pickens's oil company, Mesa Limited Partnership, pays up to $354 more a year to employees who file no medical claims, take no sick days, exercise at least thirteen times a month, and maintain appropriate weight, blood-pressure, and cholesterol levels. A Manhattan real estate company, Atco Properties and Management, pays $500 to employees who climb the sixteen flights of stairs to its offices every day for a year. And at Sara Lee, employees judged to be in excellent health are given up to $200 a year to spend on wellness-related expenses.[15]

The policy of simply providing information to people, rather than enabling them (or acting on their behalf), is not accidental; it is part of an ideology that assumes we are all independent actors, free to choose our behavior—and responsible for that behavior both morally and practically. This radical individualism derives from *laissez-faire* conservatism, libertarianism, and neoclassical social science.[16] If those subject to this ideology acknowledge any obligation at all, it is limited only to informing people of the consequences of their actions or inaction. If *individuals choose* to disregard the information, it is their funeral. The report's bias—and more generally the notion that the individual *ought* to be responsible for his or her health—is manifested in the assumption that individuals are indeed *capable* of making choices that will significantly affect their health. We shall provide evidence showing that these choices are largely made for them, and that the resources (broadly construed) that individuals would need to make effective choices are systematically denied to them. Further, we shall argue that the most effective way that individuals *can* act is precisely in the manner that the report and its attending ideology disregard: as a *community*, not as individuals; as members or citizens, not as individual consumers.

We shall show that the evidence is unmistakable that individual behavior is far more determined—"locked in"—than free. Further, we shall show that by misfocusing attention on individual action, the policies advocated by radical individualists are not only ineffective (they deflect resources and attention), but cause harm. These observations will be highlighted by examining four elements of choice: the sources of our healthy (and not so healthy) "preferences" (i.e., our objectives and desires); the sources (and lack thereof) of information necessary to make healthy decisions; the determinants of access to healthy options; and, finally, who is (are) the proper actors? That is, who has leverage over our health?

Preference Formation

Neoclassical economists and other social scientists use the term *preferences* to refer to what an individual seeks to accomplish. Unlike personal goals, which are often general and somewhat ephemeral ("Be healthy"), a preference (also referred to as a "taste") reflects a relatively specific desire: to reduce one's weight or give up smoking, for example. Given the report's assumption (shared by many other writings) that people ought to change their preferences, we need to determine how such preferences are formed and identify the forces that may modify them.

The report, and the neoclassical literature in general, does not address this critical issue. The report's implicit starting point is the notion of the autonomous individual, a person who forms her own opinions, decides what to buy and what lifestyle to pursue, and so on. The obvious roots are the social philosophy of *laissez-faire* conservatism and the neoclassical paradigm. The proponents of these twin ideological pillars assume that individuals *ought* to follow their own preferences; but they are unconcerned with how individuals came to hold such preferences. As one observer put it, neoclassicists assume that people are born at age twenty-one, with their preferences intact.

But individuals are *not* born with clear preferences to follow. Preferences are introduced by a cornucopia of voices—those of educators, peers, cultural agents, and television. Gradually, each individual evolves a personal profile from these numerous societal inputs. However, because the pressures on individuals to lean this or that way (which reach them both consciously and unconsciously) continue through adult life, and because the pressures link up with values previously acquired—and because most individuals never sort out only a singular orderly pattern of preferences—their choice behavior is typically complicated and confused, and above all, "penetrated" by outside forces.

The implication of these extraindividual forces for the matter at hand is that individual health preferences are formed to a significant extent by agents *other* than the individual. Let us examine the smoking habit, and specifically young people who are not yet addicted. First, it is unclear what "native" (if any) preferences they have in this matter. Assuming that they have a preference for a long and healthy life, *none of them should become smokers*. But peer pressure associates smoking with being sophisticated, a willingness to take risks, and other such qualities. Persuasive advertising—advertising that appeals to the subconscious—affects and modifies preferences, when it ties smoking to being youthful, sporty, and sexy.

Business understands better than both the report and other neoclassical documents how preferences are formed, as the massive advertising campaigns directed toward children attest. A Senate Select Committee on Nutrition and Human Needs reports that, on average, American children watch four hours of television every day. Wadden and Brownell[17] citing this report, write that much of television advertising seeks to "influence food preferences of children." The food industry, they observe, "recognized that food preferences can be shaped early in life"; indeed, "before most children can even talk, they recognize and reach for advertised products from their seats in the shopping carts."[18] What *type* of food is advertised? One study of more than 7,500 food commercials aimed at children found that 51 percent were for cereals, 22 percent for candy and gum, 11 percent for crackers and cookies. There was *one* commercial for vegetables.[19]

Television advertising clearly influences preferences. Wadden and Brownell observe:

> The television commercial is one of the most powerful teaching devices yet invented for placing a relatively simple message in a child's mind.

> Children under eight years of age rarely recognize that commercials are designed to promote products, and they distinguish programs from commercials only by saying that the commercials are "funnier" or "shorter." Younger children believe that there is someone inside the television talking to them, and the commercial has the quality of an order rather than a suggestion. [Numerous sources cited by the authors are omitted.][20]

Most important: TV "health" lessons translated into actual behavior:

> In one study, 516 families were observed making cereal selections in the supermarket. In two-thirds of the cases, children initiated the selection by demanding or requesting a specific brand. Children successfully influenced 85% of mothers for cereal selection, 58% for snack foods, and 40% for candy.[21]

Finally, we must consider not only the signals sent to children, but *all* health messages in the context of the commercials. The Senate committee concluded:

The television commercial is a powerful medium for influencing food preferences and food selections. Current advertising by the food industry overwhelms what few attempts there are to teach proper nutritional practices.[22]

Commercials are the most visible and easy to measure source of extraindividual effects on preferences, but they are far from the only ones. Such effects also include numerous cultural forces (e.g., fashion), religious and moral education (in the past, many considered drinking and smoking to be sinful), mobility (e.g., exposure to other societies through overseas travel), and many other societal forces.

If we ignore the effects these commercial and societal forces have on preferences, we disregard major forces that lock in ill behavior and overlook both measures for overcoming these forces and measures for developing and sustaining healthy preferences. It might be argued, for instance, that whatever progress has been made to curb smoking was largely achieved on the societal level. The government, not the free market, provided the authoritative information about the dangers of smoking; the "market" did all it could to *obscure* the preference-changing message. It was the government that pressured corporations to reduce tar and nicotine, curbed cigarette advertising, and forced the display of health warnings. Finally, changes in local ordinances stigmatized smoking and gave social support to an antismoking mentality, leading to a change in the *societal valuation* of smoking, making it less preferred.

Know Thy Options

Assuming that some have somehow evolved healthy preferences—the desire to follow a wholesome "lifestyle," to take responsibility for their health—they must then acquire information about the means to become healthy. Those who seek to avoid alcohol need to know that beer is alcoholic (many assume it is not!); those who wish to stop smoking need to know about the addictive effects of nicotine and whether secondary smoke is dangerous; those who diet should know, the caloric and salt content of various food items, and so on. Without information, healthy choices are simply impossible.

For individuals to find such information is a daunting task. There are about 25,000 items in a supermarket to choose from,[23] with more than fifty nutrients and food constituents of nutritional importance, aside from natural toxins, food additives, and significant contaminants.[24] Many combinations are new and relatively unfamiliar.

The report assumes that individuals will be able to obtain the necessary information, but never asks *how* they are to do so. While 72 percent of adult Americans knew by 1979 that sodium is the substance in food that is most often associated with high blood pressure,[25] this knowledge becomes irrelevant if food labeled "unsalted" contains other sodium compounds that are technically not salt (sodium chloride), but have the same negative effects on the body.[26] (Such chemicals give food the flavor to which consumers are accustomed; hence, they never develop a palate for truly salt-free food.) Further, 35 percent of packaged foods do not inform *at all* about their salt content,[27] especially those foods that many people assume are salt-free: cereals, frozen foods, and cold cuts. Unfortunately, such dietary information is often available only to the extent that government regulations require its disclosure and to the extent that these regulations are enforced.

For example, more than a third of the 1988 corn crop in Illinois and Iowa was tainted with aflatoxin, a highly carcinogenic fungus. In at least one case, investigators found that the level of aflatoxin was five times higher than that considered safe for human consumption. The contaminated corn was passed on to the unsuspecting consumer in products as diverse as fresh milk and cheese (grain-fed livestock), beer, cereal, corn chips, tacos, and a host of baked and processed goods.[28] Similarly, it is nearly impossible for the consumer to determine personally if the water he or she drinks is "safe"—or, for that matter, what is contained in the air he or she breathes.

Shopping for healthy food is clearly *not* like comparison shopping based on price. Gaining the necessary information could be only be done individually if each consumer were to shop with a van full of test animals; have them ingest, say, the untested chemicals in ice creams; and then wait some thirty years to establish their effects on the animals—and their offspring.

True, some positive steps have been taken recently, most notably the implementation by the Food and Drug Administration, (FDA), (along with the U.S. Department of Agriculture, (USDA)) of new labeling regulations, following the Nutritional Education and Labeling Act of 1990. Labeling requirements proposed in late 1991 would require not only certain nutritional information, but would also define uniformly such terms as natural and less.[29] Politics, however, soon entered the scene. Organizations such as the Grocery Manufacturers Association found the regulations too restrictive.[30] Then, under pressure from the Office of Management and Budget, FDA head David Kessler issued an alternative approach, weakening requirements for using the terms reduced and less. For example, under the original proposal, a product would have to have 50 percent less fat than a comparable item to claim reduced fat. Under the new proposal, fat would only have to be reduced by three grams per serving, which would be a minor reduction, for instance, in gourmet ice cream, which may have as many as 27 grams per serving. Similar changes were made in reduced-calorie and reduced-sodium claims (to the point that a salty canned soup that contains 900 milligrams of sodium could still be labeled "reduced sodium").[31] Moreover, the Agriculture Department has delayed its labeling implementation, so far, until 1994.[32]

Individuals often have difficulty assessing risks as well. What experts may deem a substantial hazard, consumers may dismiss more readily because of the public's perception of the "acceptability" of risks. Even when appropriate information is available, politics may play a role. When the Department of Agriculture proposed changing the four basic food groups to a food pyramid that deemphasized meat and dairy products, industries that deal with these foods lobbied the department to the point that publication of the new pyramid graphic was suspended.[33] But as New York University nutrition professor Marion Nestle said, "The standard four food groups are based on American agricultural lobbies. Why do we have a milk group? Because we have a National Dairy Council. Why do we have a meat group? Because we have an extremely powerful [meat lobby]."[34]

An occasional news item seems to suggest that people can be informed. For instance, an affluent citizen has periodically spent millions of dollars to place full-page ads in newspapers that call attention to the ill effects of palm oil, which is widely used by producers of cookies, crackers, and cereals.[35] The industry responded by promising to use less of this oil. But for every product "fixed" in this manner, many scores go unsettled. There are *thousands* of untested chemicals in use. We do not know if the substitutes for palm oil are healthier overall. And, unfortunately, people tire of such news, and tend to ignore it. In short, far from being able to get the information needed to act in a healthy manner, consumers are largely dependent on society for whatever information they can or cannot obtain.

Access to Healthy Alternatives

An individual with the "right" preference (e.g., to reduce sodium in his or her diet), and the necessary information (e.g., the amount of sodium in cold cuts), still needs *sources* for the preferred, healthy items (e.g., salt-free items). *Laissez-faire* ideology states that the market will provide the desired items, and if it does not, it is because people are not willing to pay enough for them. The great increase in health and natural foods sales since the rise of the health-and-fitness movement is supposedly a case in point: the market responded to demand. In fact, however, large corporations often prevent the market from working—and these are not limited imperfections, but large-scale distortions.

One distortion is the significant power that large corporations have over consumer outlets. Market shelves are crowded with brand-name products from big firms. When, rarely, a new product from a small firm becomes successful, the large corporations often integrate it into their product lines. In the process, the large firms often render the end product less healthy, in order to allow for more profitable modes of production or marketing.

Yogurt illustrates the transformation of a genuinely healthy food into a somewhat illusory one. Yogurt was the quintessential natural health food, associated with peasants and longevity. It was a wholesome product: rich in protein, calcium, and riboflavin, and low in fat, sodium, and sugar. Then the mass-production industry took it over, adding large amounts of sugar, fat, and flavoring. Now, 18 percent of the calories in La Yogurt come from fat, in Yoplait, 19 percent, and in Whitney's, 23 percent. At many outlets (especially vending machines), it is impossible to find a plain, low-fat yogurt; advertisements heavily promote the less healthy brands. Frozen yogurt is even worse. Numerous chemicals are often added, including emulsifiers and stabilizers (mono- and diglycerides, guar gum, locust bean gum, polysorbate 80, and calcium carrageenan) and artificial coloring.[36] And frozen yogurt does not usually contain live, active cultures, yogurt's most beneficial ingredient.

Another case of product transformation is tofu (soybean curd), which caught on as a product with no cholesterol, butterfat, lactose, or preservatives—and it's kosher, to boot.[37] But once the food industry began to mass-market tofu products, the amount of tofu in each of them plummeted. Tofutti, the "tofu frozen dessert," contained less than 10 percent tofu when it was studied in 1983; indeed, in some cases, there is no tofu *at all* in tofu products.[38]

The list goes on: Pepperidge Farm took vegetables, another healthy food, and marketed them under names like Mushroom Dijon and Zucchini Provencal after adding 13 to 18 grams of fat per serving—resulting in 55 to 65 percent of the calories coming from fat alone, similar to the ratio in a slice of cheesecake.[39] Granola has also been given the treatment: it has been loaded with sugars or sweeteners and unsaturated fats, yet it's still marketed as a "natural" food.[40]

Not only are health foods thus transmogrified into considerably less wholesome products, but the industry continues to play up the health theme, with little societal pressure to do otherwise: "The attorneys general [of eight states] believe the federal government has shirked its regulatory duties, permitting the country's major food marketers to position their products in possibly misleading ways—without fear of reproach."[41]

Often when consumers turn to a healthy option, industries use it to market less healthy, but more profitable, products under the same label, requiring a vigilant, ingenious, investigative consumer, with great resources, to "work" the market. An egregious example is Sara Lee's *Light* Classic desserts, which contained more calories than their regular, fattening counterparts. A Sara Lee spokesperson said that "light" referred to the "texture" of the product line, which included chocolate mousse, strawberry mousse, French cheesecake, and strawberry French cheesecake. Specifically, the Sara Lee representative explained that the products were "aerated," but not "lower in some sort of nutrition component" than other Sara Lee desserts.[42] Pursued by nine state attorneys general, Sara Lee finally agreed to stop the deceptive advertising. Even though the manufacturer paid $80,000 in investigative costs, it admitted no wrongdoing.

Cheese that is marketed as "low-fat", "light," "calorie reduced," or "lower-fat" often contains only a little less fat than the original (which is loaded). Light Vitalait, for example, weighs in at 5 grams of fat per ounce, compared to 9 in most cheddar cheeses. But that still means that 64 percent of its calories come from fat (about as much as in a sirloin steak).[43] Cream cheese gets 88 percent of its calories from fat, with its "lower fat" counterpart just seven misleading percentage points behind, at 81 percent.[44] Crackers bearing "wheat" in their wholesome-sounding names often contain large amounts of refined white flour, fat, sugar, and only minuscule portions of whole wheat. And labels that claim products are prepared with "100% vegetable oil" sometimes conceal the use of coconut and palm oils, among the most loaded with saturated fats—100 percent and 25 percent, respectively—more than lard. Sea salt, while richer in trace elements than purified regular salt, is still simply sodium chloride, even if it is sold separately (at twice the price) in the health-food section and is touted as an ingredient on many "natural foods" labels.[45]

The nation's diet industry recently promoted "all natural" fiber supplements in line with reports by the National Cancer Institute that eating more fiber could reduce the risk of colon cancer. Their labeling practices are misleading, at best. Most of these costly supplements contain scant amounts of fiber, and fiber may be found in many fruits and vegetables.

> Current labeling practices are misleading. Fibre Trim, the leading brand of supplement, for example, boasts that it contains "44 percent fiber." That sounds impressive. But it's also true that each small pill contains only a third of a gram of fiber—about the same as in a slice of white bread, and far short of the daily dose of 20 to 30 grams.[46]

Large and growing segments of the public want to buy "health," "organic," and "natural" foods, and are willing to pay more for these, according to the USDA. (The market had increased to $3.3 billion by 1983.)[47] However, since "health," "organic," and "natural" are not defined, few barriers exist to prevent industries from selling whatever they make as healthier products. The FDA protects consumers to some extent against certain false claims (e.g., that a product cures cancer), but this tends to make many assume that all advertisers' claims must be valid. But "validity" becomes a problem, because when no standard exists (e.g., what is health food?), no claim can be proved false. A move toward deterring such exploitation was the passage of legislation in 1990 that set up an Organic Standards Board, whose mandate is to define such terms. Likewise, the FDA recently insisted that reconstituted orange juice can no longer be called "fresh."

Dr. Victor Herbert, a professor of medicine at Mount Sinai School of Medicine in New York City, sums up the situation in strong terms and raises a new challenge: Are the health claims of isolated products ever justified? He writes that it amounts to "health fraud" for a product to claim to deliver "more health efficacy and safety" than "general scientific agreement" sees in the product.[48] Unless a label provides the entire truth, he continues, the result is "specious, deceptive, and misleading."[49] A typical deception he cites is the notion that good nutrition "comes from certain products, rather than as a function of the total diet."[50] While some corporations tout wheat bran to "reduce your risk of some kinds of cancer," Herbert writes that there are *no data* showing that Americans who eat wheat-bran cereal have less cancer than those who don't eat such cereal, and further, "rat research shows *more* colon cancer with too much wheat bran. . . [and] too much bran can produce deficiencies of iron, zinc, and calcium and even intestinal obstruction."[51]

Dr. Herbert further argues that labels mislead because they say "eat more bran," instead of "this product produces adequate fiber," or "eat not less than 15 or no more than 35 g. total of all assorted fibers (from a variety of grains, fruits, and vegetables) daily." As Herbert points out, the individual is no match for the corporation:

> Can the consumer recognize fraudulent concealment and consumer deception in the media? Impossible. How can the consumer intuit concealed economic interest? How can the consumer intuit omitted adverse facts fatal to the seller's message? Example: a recent issue of a magazine contains a 16-page "Special Advertising Section" designated "Nutrition Is Forever—Update 1986: Dietary Guidelines for America." Nowhere is the consumer told that the organization is a trade organization pushing pills instead of food or as a supplement for good nutrition.[52]

Included in the article is a full-page ad for "protector vitamins: vitamin E, vitamin C, beta-carotene," which tells the consumer the irrelevant literal truth that "these bodyguards help arrest harmful free radicals," and further deceives by saying, "If your diet, like that of so many people, is coming up short, consider taking protector vitamins E, C and beta-carotene." The false message: you need supplements of E, C, and beta-carotene. What are the deceptions? They are by omission. Free radicals are arrested by all carotenoids; only 10 percent of food carotenoids are beta-carotene. The "so many people" are in other countries; most Americans get all the vitamins A and C they need in their diets. Not a single case of vitamin E deficiency due to dietary inadequacy has ever been reported in a free-living American.[53]

Similarly, "moderate amounts of vitamin C, carotene and fiber may inhibit cancer. Excessive amounts may promote it."[54] Other products are misleadingly labeled "cholesterol-free." Cholesterol only occurs in animal products. Calling a vegetable oil cholesterol-free "is like labeling a drink 'wet,'" says James Heimbach, associate administrator of the Human Nutrition Information Service of the Department of Agriculture. Moreover, such a claim says nothing about saturated fat. The amount of saturated fat in vegetable and tropical oils ranges from 9 percent for safflower, to 11 percent to 27 percent for sunflower, corn, olive, soybean, peanut, and cottonseed, to the astonishing levels of 51 percent for palm, 86 percent for palm kernel, and 92 percent for coconut.[55]

It is thus evident that it is quite difficult for individual consumers to determine which foods are healthy and how to obtain them.

Harmful Side Effects

One might concede that urging individuals to improve their lifestyles, on their own rather than as a community, is the wrong focus for health-oriented efforts, but it can also be argued that individuals as consumers can surely make *some* contribution to the matter. There are, however, harmful side effects to the individualistic, neoclassical position; they are found in the deflection of resources, energy, and attention, as well as specific harms.

Wasting the energies of the private role might be referred to as "the laetrile effect." Some years ago, a debate arose over whether to allow cancer patients to take a drug called laetrile (which was made from ground apricot pits) if the patients believed that it would aid their cure. Proponents asked, "How could it *hurt*?" But health experts oppose such "treatments" because they may drain the patient's resources and attention away from potentially effective cures. Patient dollars spent on apricot pits are not available for chemotherapy; and patients who believe they have cured their cancer through laetrile will delay, if not neglect, visits to qualified physicians, resist surgery, and so on. In much the same way, the report's suggestion that the individual ought to change his or her lifestyle to remain healthy deflects resources and attention from where they might truly be effective. The billions spent, for instance, on diet foods—which are, at best, not very helpful—could be used to finance proper treatment. And the focus on individual consumer efforts deflects resources from where they are most needed: at the community level, where individuals are *members*.

Equally problematic, the neoclassical advice often causes *direct* harm of its own (as do apricot pits, which contain a potentially toxic chemical, cyanogenic glycoside) beyond draining resources. The inattention to the *actual* consequences of the steps advocated by the report is particularly troubling.

Prescriptions in areas of health other than diet provide a troubling historical background. Take the card issued by California health authorities for people to put in their wallets as a reminder to modify their lifestyles. The suggested list includes a prescription that people ought to sleep seven to eight hours. (Some reports show that sleep requirements vary greatly, and that most individuals sleep as much as they naturally need to, whatever that amount is.) We will not examine here the scientific validity of the message, but instead focus on the effects of convincing a large number of individuals that they sleep the "wrong" amount. One cannot naively assume that given such a message, millions will simply go to bed earlier, and—bingo!—sleep the "right" amount. The actual effect is that public health authorities unwittingly encourage the purchase of sleeping pills and other, possibly undesirable behaviors, just as the American notion of "a bowel movement a day" leads millions to consume laxatives to be "regular." (The profit motive and persuasive advertising are never far behind; laxative sales total a half-billion dollars a year.)

We must ask the same basic question about promoting the "proper weight," which has become a far-from-healthy American obsession. We will consider here the scientific basis for these policies—for instance, whether the health effects of naturally low weight can be achieved by people *lowering* their weight, and whether it is proper to go after the many who are overweight because of the ill effects of the few who are obese. In passing, we note that Keys's 1980 review (as cited in Wooley and Wooley) of thirteen prospective studies on obesity and mortality concluded that the risk of early death increases only at the extremes of under- and overweight, with weight having no impact on the health of women in the middle 80 percent.[56] Rather, our focus is the harmful side effects of such policies, even if their aim *is* proper.

At first blush there seems to be considerable improvement in the American diet, in the form of increased consumption of poultry, fish, low-fat milk, fresh fruits and vegetables, and less consumption of pork, red meat, eggs, coffee, and whole milk. Data show, however, that these shifts are accompanied by other behavior changes that negate at least a good part of the benefits. The resulting diet pattern can be symbolized by a teenager who consumes an oversized cookie with a Diet Coke. Blume captures the dynamics of eating less transformed to eating more:

> Body by Tab. Sweetness without calories. Pleasure without guilt. These messages exert an irresistible pull on people who yearn to be slim but love to eat. As a result, per capita use of sugar substitutes has tripled since 1975, and retailers sell about eight billion dollars worth of artificially sweetened products each year. Today, many consumers regard the diet soft drink as a virtual necessity.[57]

Moreover, Blume points out that the weight-conscious are consuming diet soft drinks and other diet foods, in *addition* to their regular intake: "Many people aren't substituting diet drinks for regular sodas; instead, they seem to be guzzling both. Between 1975 and 1985, while diet soft drink sales climbed from 29 to 106 containers per person, sales of regular soft [drinks] increased by 47 percent."[58] She adds that "the percentage of obese Americans remained roughly constant during those years."[59] The upshot of these observations, Blume notes, is that, according to researchers who analyzed data collected from thousands of women, the users of artificial sweeteners (principally saccharin) "were no more likely than nonusers to have lost weight in the course of a year; in fact, they were more likely to have *gained* weight."[60] Sixty-nine million Americans eighteen and over were consuming products that contained saccharin or aspartame, or both. This is up 60 percent since 1978, and if under eighteen-year-olds were included, the percentage would be substantially higher.[61] In behavior akin to the artificial sweetener pattern, many of the people who have shifted to consuming chicken buy it at fast-food chains, deep-fried; those who eat more salad often drench it with salad dressing, and so on. The net result? Little change in the nation's weight problem after all the dieting.

> Occasional reports of unusual success should not blind us to the fact that techniques based on insight, education, and behavior modification have a very modest success rate. We significantly change only a small minority of those we treat. These results are understandable in view of the fact that, in many cases, the obese patient has little or no abnormality of behavior to be corrected by these interventions. Although occasional studies have found overeating by the obese, the majority have found no difference in the food intakes of obese and lean infants, children, adolescents, and adults... obesity can certainly be maintained without overeating, even with undereating. This fact is simply incompatible with the concept of curing obesity by normalizing eating behavior.[62]

Moreover, based on data from the Framingham Heart Study, which involved 5,000 people for nearly forty years, the Wooleys report that

> being underweight was more dangerous than overweight, and found no relationship between fatness and mortality for women in the middle 60% of the weight range.[63]

Another physical danger involves the effects of "yo-yo dieting," the back-and-forth loss and gain of weight. Brownell[64] reports that it can "seriously distort the body's weight-regulation system. . .the more diets you go on, the harder it becomes to lose weight." He adds that, according to studies still under way, yo-yo dieting may "increase the proportion of fat-to-lean tissue on the body," and that it may also redistribute it from hips and thighs to the abdomen, "in a way that is dangerous to health."[65] Worst of all, Brownell reports, repeatedly losing and gaining weight "may increase [the] risk of heart disease."[66] He cites two studies: researchers at Northwestern University, who monitored 1,701 men over twenty-five years, found that men with the greatest weight shifts had the highest risk of sudden death from coronary heart disease; and the Framingham Heart Study, which found that while those who lost 10 percent of their body weight reduced their coronary heart disease risk by 20 percent, those who gained 10 percent increased that risk by 30 percent.

A government publication corroborates these findings, reporting that "the rhythm method of girth control" may actually be "more harmful than maintenance of a steady weight at a high level."[67] The report observes that "serum cholesterol levels are elevated during periods of weight gain, thus increasing the risk of deposition"; it adds that "we have no evidence to show that once cholesterol is deposited it can be removed by weight reduction."[68] The conclusion: "It is possible that a patient whose weight has fluctuated up and down a number of times has been subjected to more atherogenic stress than a patient with stable, though excessive weight."[69]

Yo-yo dieting has its psychological dangers as well. Wilson[70] observes that unsuccessful dieters "may develop a sense of helplessness or hopelessness about controlling their weight, may engage in self-blame, and may experience a diminished sense of self-efficacy." Psychological problems are not limited to the on-again, off-again phenomenon, however. The report encourages prejudice concerning body size; and children are under social attack by parents and peers if they are overweight. Hillel Schwartz, author of *Never Satisfied*, a history of America's obsession with dieting, cites statistics that show "some children are dieting to such

a precarious state that they are affecting their own growth. In a recent
study of nine-year-olds in San Francisco, as many as 40% were dieting.
In the 1970s the average age at which an American female began to diet
was under 14 years old."[71] Bruch concludes: "The moralistic social
pressure aggravates the inner psychological problems and conflicts of
youngsters whose weights deviate from the stereotypic picture of a
desirable figure. The pressure to be thin seems to be on the rise, and
increasingly often parents, even physicians, condone or encourage excessive thinness."[72]

Experts are already alarmed by an epidemic of eating disorders.
Gorging, craving food, anorexia and bulimic-like behaviors are noted for
chronic dieters, who suffer a range of psychological symptoms—depression, stress, self-loathing, and struggling with a loss of control. Among
college students, the Wooleys report that "of the 40% of college women
who showed anorexic-like behavior without actually being anorexic, half
reported binge-eating. Of course, eating binges which bring diets to an
abrupt end are so characteristic of overweight patients that we have
tended to see them as part of the psychopathology of obesity rather than
as a natural consequence of voluntary weight loss."[73] "The argument
here," the Wooleys conclude, "is that cultural weight obsession is in large
part responsible for the current epidemic of eating disorders."[74]

In a nation already obsessed with weight control, the report's exhor-
tation to achieve and maintain a desirable body weight gives further
sanction to the already exploitative marketers of weight-loss books,
programs, and gimmicks, while encouraging dangerous misperceptions
among nonoverweight, indeed, lean, people, especially women.

The concept of dieting, according to Stunkard, "can be criticized on
psychological grounds: going on a diet implies going off it and the
resumption of old eating habits.[75] In light of this, he rejects the concept
of "diet," and argues instead for "a gradual change in eating patterns and
a shift to foods that the patient can continue to eat indefinitely."[76]

The Center for Food Safety and Applied Nutrition, a division of the
Food and Drug Administration, cautions the approach public health
authorities should take in promoting weight loss among the general
population precisely for the findings of the 1985 National Health Interview Survey (NHIS): "There were more normal weight individuals
trying to lose weight (34.1 million) than there were overweight individuals trying to lose weight (22.6 million)."[77]

When all is said and done, one may well conclude that there is little, if any, *net* gain from a public health viewpoint, from policies that exhort individuals to diet.

Will Power: The I & We

Assume it has been established that putting certain amounts of fluoridation into drinking water significantly reduces tooth decay. There are two ways that fluoridation can be introduced: The first is to inform each individual that it is in his or her interest to use it, and then to wait for the market to provide the proper product and for people to heed the health message and use the product properly, and above all, routinely. The other is to put fluoride into the water supply (after proper examination by health authorities and the approval of elected officials). The first approach, part and parcel of the individualistic position, captures the ideology of the report and other such documents, as well as the neoclassical paradigm. The second approach is communal: *Actions are taken by the community on behalf of the members, subject to the members' guidance.* The first model is, theoretically, driven by the market; the second works via communal institutions, not necessarily the government. For example, the American Heart Association now provides in both stores and restaurants a symbol akin to the "Good Housekeeping seal" for foods low in fat, cholesterol, and sodium. I call the communal approach the *I& We approach*, to emphasize that the individual does play a role (as member, citizen, and, to some extent, consumer) and because health policy formulated independently of citizen support will not be effective, nor will it last—at least in an open, democratic society.[78]

The NHIS report ignores the communal factors and the individual's role in the community as member and citizen, and instead focuses on the individual's consumer role. Indeed, many of the "lifestyle" health messages concern individual will power—for instance, stopping smoking, saying "no" to drugs, dieting, exercising, and so on. It is also a central feature of the individualistic ideology that individuals *should* have character strength; that is the underlying meaning of "just say no" (and do what is "right").

If one approaches the same subject aware of the influence of individualistic ideology, it becomes apparent that people's will power is largely a given and that they cannot increase or enhance it; to do so requires will power. More important, the nature and extent of individual will power largely reflects social, cultural, and political forces over which individuals have little control. Thus, a person who has lost her job because the Federal Reserve increased interest rates to fight inflation and caused a recession (there were four such induced recessions between 1970 and 1982), or because of technological changes or other such "macro" reasons, will experience considerable stress, and much of her psychic energy will be expended looking for work. Under such conditions, the person is far less likely to have "enough" will power than is a person of leisure, or someone with a secure, well-paying, and meaningful job. Moreover, the level of will power reflects, in part, early childhood education (character formation), which the adult can hardly change. Do not blame the victim; change the circumstances.

In the health literature, this issue is variously discussed as a matter of *individual* "compliance," "adherence," or "implementation." The literature implicitly assumes, as does the neoclassical model, that if people choose to live "right," they will act right, as if there were no significant macro impediments that had to be removed. It has often been noted that the term compliance is authoritarian. It implies that the patient should simply follow the physician's or public health authority's advice; and it suggests that patients are neglectful of their responsibilities if they do not. Some writers have attempted to correct the term with the phrase "therapeutic alliance,"[79] for practical reasons (less resentment and hence less resistance to "advice") or ethical ones (patient dignity). However, nearly all health literature is imbedded with individualistic, voluntaristic assumptions: if the patient is willing, he or she is able, and compliance or will power can be amplified by moralistic messages. A common attitude toward noncompliance is illustrated by the use of moralistic-psychoanalytic language, which call it "self destructive behavior."[80] The report and its ideological kin essentially ignore the issue [(it is touched upon on page 513)]. This dismissal is of some significance, because even a cursory examination reveals the inability of most people to follow "change-your-lifestyle" advice most of the time. Disregarding ideological and ethical issues, it is a surprising position on technical grounds alone—akin to telling people to improve their health by lifting 250-pound weights, sitting on mountaintops, and living in large, uncrowded mansions.

The data on compliance cover relatively trivial matters as well as those that are life-threatening. Brushing one's teeth (important, but not a life-and-death matter) is favored by dentists. Of 1,000 patients followed for eight years, only 16 percent complied with suggested maintenance; 34 percent never came back. The rest of the sample complied sometimes, despite much greater tooth loss in the noncomplying proportions.[81]

Then there are the statistics on smoking:

> Out of every 100 smokers who try to quit, 60 percent go back to smoking before the year is out. . . .The rate of relapse for tobacco use appears to be very similar to that for alcohol and heroin. Surveys have shown that quitting smoking is as hard for smokers as giving up heroin is for heroin users, or giving up alcohol is for alcohol abusers. In one study conducted some years ago it was found that 40 percent of smokers, drinkers, and heroin users were still abstaining after two months, and that by the end of the first year 35 percent of the drinkers and 25 percent of the smokers and heroin users were abstaining.[82]

Less than half of all American drivers wear their seat belts although they know seat belts reduce the likelihood of death or injury in an auto accident.[83]

Many smokers continue to smoke after a heart attack although they know the dangers. The same holds for diabetics and kidney dialysis patients. Higher rates of compliance are found in taking some medications, especially in the first year (some studies report initial rates as high as 94 percent); but these do not entail changes in lifestyle.

One of the very few who called attention to this matter is an outstanding sociologist, one of the experts on health behavior, David Mechanic. He wrote, in 1979, "We know relatively little about the way people develop healthful patterns of behavior . . . thus severely limiting our ability to develop models for intervention."[84] Mechanic then takes the important step to call attention to the fact that the patterns of behavior involved are "deeply embedded in early childhood development, culture, and life situations." He adds that the factors involved are often *not* under the patient's control. The very term lifestyle reflects the illusion; it implies that it is something that can be changed as readily as one's hairstyle or style of dress, or even one's writing style. Actually, the main seat of constraints and of action is communal; there is relatively little an individual can achieve on her own. She can serve her health best by acting as a member of the community and the polity (by supporting proper communal actions and opposing unhealthy ones) rather than as an individual consumer.

The web of communal forces is complex. It includes shared values, language, culture, economic institutions, and government. An analysis of the role of these factors in determining our health remains largely to be written. Here we focus on one key matter: the role of the individual as a member (and citizen) as distinct from a consumer.

People must recognize that all policies—including those concerning matters such as airline safety, environmental protection, and health—are made in public arenas, that is, are subject to power relations. For instance, early reports on dieting goals for Americans were attacked by several commodities industries (dairy, egg, and cattle).[85]

The New York Times,[86] in a story similar to many others, reported that the Agriculture Department had proposed allowing prepared meats such as hot dogs to contain "as much as 10 percent ground bone and other remnants from a mechanical process without identifying the ingredients in product labels." The use of such "salvaged remnants" was approved for some foods in 1978, but according to the *Times*, "the industry complained that the stricter initial regulations called too much attention to the finely ground bone and that [therefore] the product failed to gain widespread use." It seems clear that one reason such labeling is voluntary rather than mandatory, often inadequate, and confusing (if not downright misleading) is the political pressure against it.[87]

There is no shortage of examples of political power playing a key role in health matters, from the struggle to undercut the FDA, to the role of the alcohol lobby in fighting enhanced penalties on drunken drivers, to the role of tobacco states and lobbies in challenging the evidence on smoking's health risks. Behind these major political powers lie a slew of smaller ones. One example, reported by Dr. Victor Herbert,[88] will have to suffice. It concerns a trade organization of vitamin and mineral supplement producers that conceals its economic interest from the public and sells $5 billion in dietary supplements using deceptive advertising. These producers highlight irrelevant truths and withhold adverse facts— for example, labeling toxic doses of a product as "superpotent." Herbert observes[89] that "'superpotent' is truthful but deceptive advertising jargon for 'toxic.'" Herbert reports that in 1980, the organization influenced a federal judge to forbid an FDA warning label on very-low-calorie diets (VLCDs), products that were being sold directly to the public by some of its member firms. These diets, which prescribe less than 900 calories per day, cannot be directly sold to the public in Canada—and for good reason. Herbert concludes that the result of the judge's ruling was "an unknown number of deaths, which some of the surviving next of kin alleged in lawsuits against the manufacturers and others were due to the VLCDs."[90]

The health matters are, to a significant extent, not decided at checkout counters in supermarkets, kitchen counters, or fast-food outlets, but on the public level. Hence, only if members of the community support the needed public health policies and measures against opposing forces will they generate the required political energy for health. These policies and measures, discussed below, can in part be introduced into the market system (e.g., more and better labels). In other instances, they require community action, regulation, or public provision, say, of healthy drinking water. The whole situation may be illustrated by a person who washes a red apple before consuming it, not realizing that it is laced with a strong carcinogen. Even if the person knew, there is nothing he or she could do about it, short of throwing the apple out. And the same holds true for countless other products; milk, lettuce. The only realistic means to improve health is for carcinogenic and otherwise harmful substances (i.e., food additives and "naturally harmful" foods, modes of preparation and marketing) to be condemned by the community, avoided by industry, and—if need be—banned by the government.

What Can We Do?

We must politicize health. In fact, we must recognize that it is already highly politicized. It is no accident that 39 percent of the foods in the marketplace have no labels on them at all.[91] Such practices reflect the relative strength of various farm and trade lobbies and the relative weakness of various civic groups (Naderites, for example), combined with whatever support the public gives to reform. Because of the relative power of the respective industry lobbies and their allies in Washington, federal taxes on hard liquor have increased very little over the years, and federal taxes on beer and wine have not been raised since 1951[92].

People who care about their health, the health of their loved ones, and the health of the next generation of Americans must understand that health is not a *private* matter between them, their physician, the gym, and the bathroom scale. It is, to a significant extent, a reflection of a tug-of-war between those who promote ill factors (usually simply in the pursuit of more profit, power, and continuation of tradition) and the small band of those who resist them. Most important, the political forces that undergird the present unhealthy factors will not budge unless major new sources of political energy are unleashed and a new force arises. This cannot be generated by individuals acting on their own; the system only responds to what political scientists call aggregation, the coming together of numerous people to support the needed policies, institutional changes, and reforms. By far the most effective way to improve individual health is to stand at the ballot box instead of the bathroom scale. This is not a call for a life of self-denial or altruism. It is a recognition that one's deepest personal needs, for life and health, are best served by *community* action. Here there is no contradiction between self-interest and sharing. Thus, when we find out which politician is bought by the nursing-home lobby, and which voluntary association we can join with confidence (AARP?), our most narrow self-interest *and* that of our fellow citizens are jointly served. Since health is indivisible, the shortest route to significantly improving our individual health, paradoxically, is the community way, and trying to serve oneself while ignoring others is self-defeating.

Reasonable people can differ about the nature of the communal approach to health. Old-fashioned liberals may favor direct action by government agencies; for example, the Department of Agriculture could open stores that would sell only truly healthy food. At the very least, these liberals would like to see more government regulations and inspection, and severe penalties for those who violate or evade health regulations.

For instance, liberals want all foods to be marked with coherent and usable nutrition information. Instead of a long list of highly technical terms and difficult-to-compare gram measurements, liberals want to see consumer-friendly pie charts that will reveal by the size of the slices the hidden truths about total and relative fat, carbohydrates, and salt. They want the new labels to be combined with a new requirement for standard definitions of slippery terms such as "light" and "natural." These ideas found a home in the Nutrition Labeling and Education Act sponsored by Congressman Henry Waxman of California and Senator Howard Metzenbaum of Ohio. The bill requires that, in addition to the new nutrition labeling and definitions of health and disease prevention claims, grocers post information or distribute brochures concerning the nutritional aspects of fresh fruits, vegetables, and fish.[93]

Liberals also want more government control of advertising. Like so many other regulatory agencies, the Federal Trade Commission (FTC), in charge of prosecuting deceptive advertisers and protecting consumers, suffered from Reagan's budget cuts. Under the former commissioner of the FTC there were 1,000 major commission decisions in a six-month period. In a recent half-year there were only 109[94]. To fill the void left by the emaciated FTC, many state attorneys general have decided to take the controls and have already proved more aggressive and efficient at catching violators.

Finally, liberals may also support closer government inspection. The Department of Agriculture recently reported that up to 35 percent of the chicken sold in U.S. stores is infected with salmonella (reported by Public Voice for Food and Health Safety).[95] Between January and November of 1989 there were 1,628 cases of salmonellosis reported, compared to 608 in all of 1985.[96] This may mean only nausea, fever, and vomiting for many; but thirteen people died from the poisoning during those months (compared to one in 1985). Seafood, which is sixteen times more likely to cause an outbreak of illness than poultry, is not subject to mandatory safety inspection at all.[97] A study by Consumers Union of seafood in New York City and Chicago found widespread contamination and mislabeling. Of the 113 samples studied, 34 were spoiled, 50 were contaminated with fecal coliform, and one-third were misidentified.[98] Improving food safety does not require more legislation; all that is needed is more inspectors and heftier penalties for violators. A National Academy of Sciences report points to the kind of inspection that is needed. It argues that inspection during processing is less likely to detect contamination than monitoring the waters where the fish were caught. The report also contended that the present methods used by the Department of Agriculture—smelling, feeling, and looking at the seafood—cannot detect many health hazards, such as viruses, natural toxins, bacteria, and man-made chemicals.[99]

Neoliberals look to market incentives that encourage industries to focus greater attention on public health. For example, the government might encourage organic farming by promising to buy "clean" produce for the armed forces. It could also encourage farmers not to use pesticides by offering tax credits and other financial incentives. Another market strategy might sound like this: "When Coke airs an ad for their product," suggests Bonnie Liebman, the director of nutrition at the Center for

Science in the Public Interest, "they should be required to spend a comparable amount for public service announcement air time encouraging healthful eating."[100]

Communitarians will call on voluntary associations to help us select healthy items on supermarket shelves and on restaurant menus. For years, the American Heart Association has been working with restaurants throughout the country, marking their menus with signs of approval next to those dishes that pass the scrutiny of the AHA's dietitians, who review the recipes for fat, cholesterol, and sodium content.[101]

Other communitarians may want to support public interest groups. The Consumer Pesticide Project of the National Toxics Campaign recently negotiated an agreement with six major supermarket chains in the United States and Canada whereby the chains promise to phase out their stocks of foods laden with cancer-causing pesticides.[102] Thus, consumers need not examine thousands of individual products, but can, in effect, rely on the supermarket to be their agent, while consumer watchdogs ensure that the stores live up to their promises.

Combined action on all fronts is probably needed if we are to improve our health significantly. The forces that profit from unhealthy conditions (or from not having to attend to them) are deeply entrenched. It will take a major public mobilization to dislodge them and make room for the needed health measures.

Americans have made one decision already. We now define the good life not simply as one that is longer; we wish our longer life span to be one of *quality* years, not years crippled with illness. But we have yet to learn that just as it is more effective to have the proper amount of fluoridation in the town's water supply rather than adding it daily in one's kitchen, so in most matters concerning citizens' well-being we are no match for the system as isolated individuals. We are the body social; we can make that body healthier and through it secure our own health.

Notes

1. U.S. Department of Health and Human Services, Public Health Service, The Surgeon General's Report on Nutrition and Health Summary and Recommendations, DHHS Washington, DC: U.S. Government Printing Office, 1988, 1.
2. J. H. Knowles, "The Responsibility of the Individual," in *Doing Better and Feeling Worse: Health in the United States* (New York: Norton, 1977), 58.
3. Ibid., 59.

4. J. A. Califano, Jr., Healthy People: The Surgeon General's Report on Health Promotion and Disease Prevention, Washington, DC: U.S. Government Printing Office, 1979, viii.

5. Ibid.

6. Joseph D. Matarazzo et al., eds. *Behavioral Health: A 1990 Challenge for the Health Sciences* (New York: Wiley, 1984), 16.

7. Ibid, 21.

8. Benjamin Blech, "Don't Blame the Victim," Newsweek, September 19, 1988, 10.

9. Ibid.

10. Alfred E. Harper, "Nutrition: From Myth and Magic to Science," *Nutrition Today*, 23, 1 (January/February 1988):8-17.

11. Richard Evans, "Health Promotion—Science or Ideology?" Health Psychology 7, 3 (1988):207.

12. Kenneth B. Noble, "Company Halting Health Plan on Some 'Life Style' Illnesses," *The New York Times*, August 6, 1988, A1.

13. Glenn Kramon, "Business and Health: New Incentives to Take Care," *The New York Times*, March 21, 1989, D2.

14. Mary Rowland, "Matching Life Styles to Benefits," *The New York Times*, March 1, 1992, 14 (from a survey by Foster Higgins released in January 1992).

15. Claudia H. Deutsch, "Rewarding Employees for 'Wellness,'" *The New York Times*, September 15, 1991, 21.

16. See Amitai Etzioni, *The Moral Dimension: Toward a New Economics* (New York: The Free Press, 1988).

17. Thomas A. Wadden and Kelly D. Brownell, "The Development and Modification of Dietary Practices in Individuals, Groups, and Large Populations," in *Behavioral Health*, Matarazzo et al., eds. 608-631.

18. Ibid., 612.

19. Ibid., 613.

20. Ibid.

21. Ibid.

22. Ibid.

23. Lena Williams, "Free Choice: When Too Much Is Too Much," *The New York Times*, February 14, 1990, C1.

24. D. M. Hegsted, "What Is a Healthful Diet?" in Behavioral Health, Matarazzo et al., eds., 552.

25. Alan Levy and Tanya Guthrie, Prevalence and Distribution of Sodium-Avoidance Dieting Behavior in the United States: 1982-1988, Washington, DC: FDA Division of Consumer Studies, 1989, 10.

26. Chris W. Lecos, A Consumer's Guide to Food Labels. (HHS Publication No. 85-2083), Rockville, MD: FDA Division of Consumer Services, Department of Health and Human Service, 1985.

27. Mary Bender, Status of Nutrition and Sodium Labeling on Processed Foods: 1988, Washington, DC: FDA Division of Consumer Studies, 1989, 5.

28. Scott Kilman, "Abstracts," *The Wall Street Journal*, February 23, 1989, 1.

29. Philip J. Hilts, "U.S. Will Propose New Restrictions on Food Labeling," *The New York Times*, November 6, 1991, A1.

30. Marian Burros, "In Switch, F.D.A. Offers Looser Rules on Labels," *The New York Times*, February 11, 1992, A16.

31. Editorial, "Why Cave on Honest Food Labels?" *The New York Times*, February 25, 1992, 20.

32. Bruce Ingersoll, "U.S. to Delay Enforcing Plan to Relabel Meat," *The Wall Street Journal*, March 19, 1992, B1.
33. Laura Shapiro et al., "Feeding Frenzy," *Newsweek*, May 27, 1991, 49.
34. Ibid.
35. Advertisement, "The Poisoning of America!," *The New York Times*, April 4, 1990, A21.
36. Bonnie Liebman, "Noveau Junk Food: Consumers Swallow the Back-to-Nature Bunk," *Business and Society Review* (Fall 1984):48–50.
37. Marc Medoff, "Tofutti's Little Secret," *Nutrition Action Health Letter*, Center for Science in the Public Interest, 1986, 10.
38. Ibid.
39. Liebman, "Noveau Junk Food," 48–49.
40. Ibid.
41. Carol Sugarman, "The New Chow Hounds," *The Washington Post*, September 21, 1988, E1.
42. Ibid.
43. Tufts University Diet and Nutrition Letter 6, 10, December 1988, 7.
44. Leni Reed, "Milk's Leap - into Cheese," American Health, September 1988, 96.
45. Bonnie Liebman, "5 of the Best & 5 of the Worst Buys in the Natural Foods Supermarket," Nutrition Action Health Letter, November 1984, 11.
46. "Truth in Fiber," *The New York Times*, June 26, 1988, 26 E.
47. Sam Zuckerman, "The Natural Facts," *Nutrition Action Health Letter,* November 1984, 5.
48. Victor Herbert, "Health Claims in Food Labeling and Advertising: Literal Truths but False Messages; Deception by Omission of Adverse Facts," *Nutrition Today* 22, 3 (May/June, 1987):25.
49. Ibid.
50. Ibid.
51. Ibid.
52. Ibid., 28.
53. Ibid., 29.
54. Ibid., 26.
55. *U.S. News and World Report*, August 8, 1988, 60.
56. Susan C. Wooley and Orland W. Wooley, "Should Obesity Be Treated at All?" *Eating and Its Disorders*, A. J. Stunkard, and E. Stellar eds. (New York: Raven Press, 1984), 186.
57. Elaine Blume, "Do Artificial Sweeteners Help You Lose Weight?" *Nutrition Action Health Letter,* 1987, 3.
58. Ibid., 4.
59. Ibid.
60. Ibid.
61. Chris W. Lecos, Sweetness Minus Calories = Controversy, (HHS Publications No.85-2205) Rockville, MD: FDA Division of Consumer Studies, Department of Health and Human Services, 1985.
62. Wooley and Wooley, "Should Obesity Be Treated?" 185–86.
63. Ibid., 186.
64. Kelly Brownell, "The Yo-Yo Trap," American Health, March 1988, 80.
65. Ibid.
66. Ibid.

67. U.S. Department of Health, Education and Welfare, Obesity and Health: A Source Book of Current Information for Professional Health Personnel, Arlington, VA: U.S. Government Printing Office, 1966, 40.

68. Ibid.

69. Ibid.

70. G. Terence Wilson, "Weight Control Treatments," in *Behavioral Health*, Matarazzo et al., eds. New York, 667.

71. Hillel Schwartz, "Being Thin Isn't Always Being Happy," *U.S. News and World Report*, February 9, 1987, 74.

72. H. Bruch, "Developmental Considerations of Anorexia Nervosa and Obesity," *Canadian Journal of Psychiatry* 26, (1981): 212. p.

73. Wooley and Wooley, "Should Obesity Be Treated?" 188–89.

74. Ibid., 190.

75. Albert J. Stunkard, "The Current Status of Treatment for Obesity in Adults," in Eating and Its Disorders, Stunkard and Stellar, eds. *Eating and Its Disorders*, 167.

76. Ibid.

77. Marilyn G. Stephenson et al., 1985 NHIS Findings: Nutrition Knowledge and Baseline Data for Weight-Loss Objectives, Public Health Reports, vol. 102, no. 1, 1987, 63.

78. Etzioni, *The Moral Dimension*.

79. Thomas G. Wilson, "Compliance: A Review of the Literature with Possible Applications to Periodontics," Journal of Periodontology, 58, no.10 (October 1987):706.

80. Ibid., 709.

81. Ibid.

82. U.S. Department of Health and Human Services, Smoking, Tobacco and Health, Washington, DC: U.S. Government Printing Office, (revised 1989), 7–8.

83. U.S. Department of Transportation, National Highway and Traffic Safety Administration, Occupant Protection Trends in 19 Cities Washington, DC: NHTSA, 1990.

84. David Mechanic, "The Stability of Health and Illness Behavior: Results from a 16-Year Follow-Up," *American Journal of Public Health*, 69, no. 11 (November 1979):1142.

85. Wadden and Brownell, "Development and Modification of Dietary Practices," 609.

86. *The New York Times*, September 13, 1988, A28.

87. J. Mayer, "Labeling," in *U.S. Nutrition Policies in the Seventies*, J. Mayer, ed. (San Francisco: Freeman, 1973).

88. Herbert, "Health Claims in Food Labeling and Advertising," 25–30.

89. Ibid., 28.

90. Ibid.

91. Bender, "Status of Nutrition and Sodium Labeling," Table 1.

92. *Internal Revenue Code*, 1990, sec. 5042.

93. *The Wall Street Journal*, May 17, 1990, B1.

94. *The Wall Street Journal*, April 17, 1989.

95. "Dirty Chicken," *The Atlantic* November 1990, 32–49.

96. *The Wall Street Journal*, January 9, 1990, A16.

97. *CPSN Newsletter*, Consumer Product Safety Network, Winter 1989–1990, 1.

98. Marian Burros, "Study of Retail Fish Markets Finds Wide Contamination and Mislabeling," *The New York Times*, January 16, 1992, A21.

99. Susan Okie, "Seafood Safety Regulation Called Inadequate," *The Washington Post*, January 9, 1991, A3.

100. Liebman, *Business and Society Review*, 49.

101. *Restaurants USA*, October 30, 1987.
102. *Phoenix Gazette*, September 13, 1989.

6

An Alternative to Reregulation

Moral Conduct in an Unregulated Economy

The secretary of an executive at Donallco, a California corporation, reported that when she scheduled her boss to fly on an airline (she cannot remember the name), he told her to change the reservation. When she asked why, he exclaimed: "We make parts for those planes, and I am not flying on that plane."[1] The Donallco Corporation specialized in the production of bogus aircraft parts.[2] Such parts, according to study commissioned by the Federal Aviation Administration (FAA), are "a serious safety problem."[3] (Not all of them are attributable to the said corporation; it is not the only source of such parts.) Incidents like this, coming on top of the savings-and-loan (S&L), crisis and frequent scandals among defense contractors, medical laboratories, and the like, have led to a movement demanding various kinds of reregulation or new regulation. To combat deficiencies in the quality of tests performed in medical laboratories, Congress passed a law in 1988 that regulates the operation of more than 300,000 laboratories.[4] Licensing, periodic inspections, and proficiency testing are required, and doctors will need to hire trained licensed technicians instead of the nurses and secretaries who now perform many of the lab tests.

To tighten corporate auditing, regulations now before Congress require that if auditors note certain irregularities, they must submit a report to the company, which, in turn, is responsible for notifying the Securities and Exchange Commission (SEC). Should the company fail to do so, the auditors will be required to submit their report to the regulators.[5]

Several proposals have been advanced that would further regulate banking practices. These include tying deposit insurance to the riskiness of banks' investments, which would greatly restrict the types of investments that banks can make (for example, limiting them to low-risk ventures) and would double or triple their deposit-insurance premiums.[6]

The business community, the Republican administration, most economists, and many others in the public at large are troubled by this trend toward more regulation. They basically hold that regulations are tantamount to government meddling, and the less meddling, the better for all concerned.

What, if anything, is needed to replace regulation? The business community is surprisingly mum on this question. Occasionally, its representatives argue that no particular steps are needed because markets and, more generally, economic conduct are self-correcting. If a supplier produces shoddy products—items that maim workers or endanger consumers, for example—people will cease to buy these items and the suppliers will go out of business. Or, the insurance premiums that suppliers would have to pay to guard against potential liability suits would be so high as to make unethical business unprofitable. Indeed, the anticipation of economic "penalties" is said to be so severe as to discourage manufacturers, sellers, and other participants in the market from acting immorally; its ethical nature is self-sustaining.

Unfortunately, this is simply not the case. There are many reasons unethical and even outright illegal behavior pays and is surprisingly common. Some conduct, such as insider trading, does not have clear, immediate victims, but slowly erodes general confidence in the markets.[7] Years pass before the word spreads that certain products are unsafe, and meanwhile manufacturers rake in high profits (for example, the manufacturers of breast implants). Nursing homes that have been caught after years of shortchanging their patients are often fined small amounts compared to what they have gained. If a home has acquired a poor reputation over the years, it may open under a different name in a neighboring state. People who take medications that are deleterious have a hard time discerning what exactly has caused their declining condition, and so on. For the market to work as expected, information would have to travel fast and free and be properly and quickly absorbed. But as the examples just cited illustrate, and many other socio-economic studies have shown, information often travels slowly, at much cost, is difficult to absorb, and is often incorrectly ingested. It follows that if reregulation is to be minimized, the integrity of the market will have to rely on some other forces than "Let the buyer beware."

Clearly, markets do not cleanse themselves, because otherwise unethical and illegal conduct would not be so rampant. Reference is not to marginal technical violations of some obscure law, but to systematic gross violations, such as those of laboratories that systematically charge for tests they did not complete and then report to physicians that all is well. Reference is not to isolated incidents of some devious firms engaging in such behavior, but to massive involvement, such as the following: the Resolution Trust Corporation, which was established to manage the S & L bailout, reports that criminal fraud was discovered in 60 percent of the savings institutions seized by the government in 1989.[8] A General Accounting Office report, issued April 26, 1990, found that about 52 percent of the gasoline it sampled in Michigan was labeled with a higher octane level than it actually contained.[9] The Inspector General's office in the Department of Defense reports that 20 of the 100 largest defense contractors were convicted in criminal cases between 1983 and 1990.[10] A study by the Department of Justice that looked at almost 600 of the largest U.S. publicly owned manufacturing, wholesale, retail, and service corporations with annual sales of $300 million or more showed that during 1975 and 1976 "over 60 percent had at least one enforcement action initiated against them [actions were all federal—administrative, civil, and criminal]. . . more than 40 percent of the manufacturing corporations engaged in repeated violations."[11]

These reports feed into the reregulation movement. (The fact that many other economies are less scrupulous, not only in the Third World but in Japan, is beside the point; Americans seem to demand a higher level of integrity from U.S. corporations.) To put it differently: business requires public acceptance. If it loses legitimacy, if the public considers business no longer properly conducted and morally sound, it will force new government controls from whomever is in the White House, Congress, or the judiciary. While some reregulation may be necessary, most would agree that it would be better all around if business would raise its level of integrity without being made to do so.

The Needed Self-Corrections

To encourage moral behavior, the business community should (1) foster associations and enforce moral codes somewhat like those of lawyers and physicians; (2) encourage business leaders to place integrity higher on their agenda; and (3) prevail upon business schools to expand the moral education of executives. Of necessity, these three major reforms are discussed one at a time. Their efficacy, however, relies heavily on their being advanced more or less simultaneously, so that they may reinforce one another.

Associations

When I served as the staff director of a commission investigating nursing homes in New York State, many demanded more government regulation of that industry. The commission was appointed after months of reports of gross abuses in largely proprietary (profit-making) nursing homes. Owners were said to have diverted funds allocated to buy their patients' food and medicines to buy themselves rare paintings and luxury cars. The homes were understaffed, and the elderly were being drugged to make them more easily manageable. As the commission prepared public hearings, I invited the heads of ten major corporations for a private discussion. I told their representatives that the commission wished to learn what could be done by the business community itself to curb abuses. After all, I pointed out, other professions, such as law and medicine, have their own associations, codes of ethics, and enforcement mechanisms. Could the managers of business also act as a professional association and help weed out the kind of people who were leading abusers in the nursing-home industry?

It was like giving a party to which nobody came. The business community, at least those with whom I spoke at the time, was not interested. But, my experience illustrates a much broader phenomenon. Lawyers and physicians define what is proper and improper conduct, and have some mechanisms—however weak and inadequate—for encouraging members to behave. And, at least occasionally, they do expel or disbar the most extreme abusers, giving some bite to their associational voice. Accountants, too, now have a code of conduct. But most business associations have no such codes and none has an enforcing mechanism. (The National Association of Manufacturers has a broad statement on good business practices but no enforcement mechanism. The Business Roundtable issued a statement in 1988 on business ethics; however, it called for actions by corporations—not the Business Roundtable.) *No-*

body ever gets kicked out, however much they may gouge the public—or one another.

True, business people are different. They need no specific license to practice, and hence even if business executives were to treat themselves as a profession, they would not have the same power as medical societies or bar associations. It does not follow, however, that business associations have no powers, or that there aren't ways to augment them once the associations make shoring up their ethics part of their endeavors. There is nothing to prevent the Business Roundtable, the Chamber of Commerce, the National Association of Manufacturers, the Conference Board, and other such bodies from conversing with their members, establishing what they consider to be proper moral conduct, and forming their own moral codes. The deliberations themselves would be sure to have some salutary effects, and so would the codes.

These codes could be given more weight if, like doctors, the business associations or yet-to-be-formed committees on business ethics would take a "walk in the woods" with CEOs of corporations that are known to be particularly errant (grievously engaged in industrial espionage, midnight dumping of toxic waste, falsified tests of medical drugs, and so on). Being expelled from the Business Roundtable, in extreme cases, would be certain to get a company's (and the market's) attention. True, it would not prevent the corporation from doing business the way, say, a disbarred lawyer might be, but the social and economic penalties are likely to be substantial.

Although not all corporations are members of these bodies, most are members of one body or another, and those that are not would come under some pressure to join were associations to become active on the side of ethics. Companies that did not join, somewhat like accountants that are not members of the American Institute of Certified Public Accountants, would come under extra scrutiny from one and all, because not belonging to some association that has and sustains a code of ethics could become a mark for clients to beware.

If business associations were inclined to move even further in the direction of professionalization, they could make lists available to federal, state, and local government agencies of censured and disbarred corporations. These agencies, in turn, would be unlikely to award contracts to such corporations. If these same lists were to be made available to not-for-profit organizations such as schools, hospitals, and colleges, the bite of the associational code would be further enhanced. Finally, corporations may find it difficult to justify to their shareholders doing business with companies that are defined as unethical by their own associations. When all is said and done, even if only a few corporations were censured or disbarred each year, it would go a long way to shoring up integrity.

This approach, however, assumes that the association's codes are based on extensive dialogues among the members and are not introduced arbitrarily. The acts of censure and disbarment are but the rough cutting edge of such a method. It is essential, as in all moral systems, to gain the voluntary compliance of most members because they perceive the code to be morally compelling and necessary if business is to maintain its legitimacy. Now, with no clear or even unclear characterization of what their peers consider improper and intolerable behavior, business communities offer little guidance in moral matters.

Leadership

If one examines changes in the moral orientations of other groups that have affected the public mind regarding what it considers legitimate—such as the neoconservative, environmental, and suffrage movements—at the forefront were inspirational leaders. These are leaders who championed new directions and built up moral support for the changes in perspectives and values. Actually, the very first were often intellectuals, writers, and editors, as different from each other as Irving Kristol is from Rachel Carson and Ralph Nader. Once their voices were heard and their messages disseminated, however, their new definitions of the problems and characterizations of what is to be done were picked up by community leaders, leaders of one segment or another of the population (e.g., women), and course-setting political leaders (e.g., John F. Kennedy).

When it comes to business ethics, while there has in recent years been a significant increase in the attention paid by academics and other intellectuals to the need to shore up integrity (by no means limited to the left and other traditional critics of business), the next stage has not taken place. With rare exceptions, voices that are influential within the business community have not made strengthening the moral fiber of business a significant theme of their concerns. Business leaders speak up against deficits, government intervention, the crisis in schools, and many other subjects, but rarely about following a higher pathway of conduct within their own profession. On the contrary, they often dismiss reports about extensive illegal and unethical conduct with statements such as: "Many, if not most, organizations are composed of morally and ethically honorable people who genuinely try to comply with the law."[12] They claim that if transgressions do occur, it is frequently because of some "rogue employee's misstep,"[13] or because "compliance with our laws is not always a simple and precise task,"[14] and thus unintentional violations may occur in even the most conscientious corporations.

Before a major movement of self-reform can take place, these leaders need to find their moral voice and address their own communities. A few mavericks who have spoken up provide an indication of what needs saying. For example:

> We as business leaders must convince the American people that we are committed to highly ethical behavior, on both a personal and corporate level. This does not call for a new public-relations strategy. Instead, we need to demonstrate our commitment to instituting practical programs to preserve the integrity of our employees and our firms.... The only way to achieve a corporate climate in which ethics becomes a part of everyday decision-making is to start at the top.[15]

From another business leader:

> I've heard business people say that we should operate honestly and ethically even though doing so makes it harder to do business. I have news for them: they're wrong. Operating honestly and ethically makes it easier to do business. I'll go even further than that, ethical conduct—and the feeling of trust that results—is the basis of successful business; in fact, it is the basis of our free American socio-economic system.... We must compete in the arena of values—not efficiency, productivity, or performance. The public already assumes that. We should show ourselves as decent human beings—not anonymous companies, but people who are honest, ethical, and concerned with the public good. We should not only be honest and ethical, we should be known to be so.[16]

The 1988 Business Roundtable's report on business ethics and the role of management states:

> In the experience of these companies with regard to corporate ethics, no point emerges more clearly than the crucial role of top management. To achieve results, the Chief Executive Officer and those around the CEO need to be openly and strongly committed to ethical conduct, and give constant leadership in tending and renewing the values of the organization. Companies find it necessary to communicate that commitment in a wide variety of ways—in directives, policy statements, speeches, company publications, and especially in actions.[17]

Most business leaders, however, have yet to be heard from on this issue.

Moral Education

Last but not least, individual members of the business community must be reached. Ideally, moral education starts at home and is reinforced by one's school, peers, neighbors, and churches.[18] Given the sorry state of American families, however, many of them are not sufficiently intact to provide effective education, especially moral education. Single parents or married couples come home after an exhausting day at work to do household chores, often having little time or energy to deal with psychologically taxing matters such as questioning their children's conduct, helping them choose proper peers, and so on. A pop psychology literature provides parents with further assurances that they need not intervene. As a result, schools are increasingly becoming the teachers of moral education, as difficult and controversial as this is.

Business schools must pick up the slack as well, because those who come through their doors often have insufficient moral education or believe that business people must leave their values behind. Several business schools have always had some courses in ethics; in recent years, their numbers have increased. Other business schools have expanded and strengthened their ethics education. Still, most students graduate from business school with very little moral preparation. This is a major area in which shoring up is needed.

Ultimately, the purpose of business associations, codes, leadership, and education is not simply to retard reregulation. Reregulation is the symptom, not the underlying cause. What is needed is to maintain the legitimacy of business, by enhancing its ethical conduct and either rehabilitating or isolating those members who undermine the social acceptance of all business, to the detriment of both business and society.

Notes

1. Transcript of "60 Minutes," May 20, 1990, 4.
2. Ibid.
3. Ibid., 7
4. The Clinical Laboratory Improvement Amendment of 1988 (CLIA); "Fierce Clash over Regulating Doctors' Office Labs," *The Washington Post*, September 18, 1990.
5. *The Wall Street Journal*, September 14, 1990.

6. "Banking's Reins: Too Tight and Too Loose," *The New York Times*, December 17, 1990, D1.
7. See James B. Stewart, *Den of Thieves* (New York: Simon & Schuster, 1991).
8. *The New York Times*, April 12, 1990, 1.
9. *The New York Times*, April 27, 1990, A13.
10. *National Journal*, April 21, 1990, 961–62.
11. Marshall B. Clinnard, *Illegal Corporate Behavior* (Washington, DC: U.S. Department of Justice, 1979).
12. Testimony of John Borgwardt of Boise Cascade Corporation before U.S. Sentencing Commission, February 14, 1990.
13. Robert J. Giuffra, "Sentencing Corporations," *The American Enterprise*, May/June 1990, 85.
14. Testimony of James Carty of the National Association of Manufacturers before the House Subcommittee on Criminal Justice, May 24, 1990.
15. Statement by Edward L. Hennessy, Jr., chairman and chief executive officer, Allied-Signal.
16. Statement by Robert V. Krikorian, chairman, Rexnord.
17. The Business Roundtable, "Corporate Ethics: A Prime Business Asset," February 1988, 4.
18. Ben Wildavsky, "Can You *Not* Teach Morality in Public Schools?" *The Responsive Community* 2 (Winter 1991/92):46–55.

7

Socio-Economics: Select Policy Implications

Socio-economics is a new paradigm that emerges out of many works that seek to combine the kind of variables typically encompassed by neoclassical economics with those contained in other social sciences (for example, the works of Albert Hirschman, Harvey Leibesinte, Herbert Simon, and Amatalia Sen). It does not so much seek to replace the kind of analysis associated with neoclassical economics (and found these days also in other branches of the social sciences such as exchange sociology and Public Choice political science), but to encompass these works in a broader framework, one that systematically adds to the study of institutions, values, and emotions that of markets, rationality, and choice behavior.[1] While socio-economics is clearly less parsimonious than new classical analysis, it claims to be able to predict and explain better, as well as stand on firm ethical grounds—claims that are not evaluated here. Instead, the discussion focuses on the kinds of policy analysis, suggestions, and insights the new paradigm leads to. In the process, these are compared with those provided by neoclassical analysis.

Because socio-economics is a new discipline, we often need to indicate not only what it recommends, but the lines of research needed to support further the suggested lines of policy analysis. A quick example will serve to illustrate this approach. Neoclassical works in labor economics that summarize the state of the art often discuss efforts to increase incentives for work performance. These books focus almost exclusively on monetary incentives such as differences between wages and salaries, pay-for-time versus piecemeal pay, and so on.[2] Socio-economics adds to such analyses the concept of reference groups, that is, the observation that people are also concerned with their relative (or nominal) wages, not only with their absolute (or real) ones.[3] The same may be said about recognizing the *intrinsic* appeal of work versus leisure, employees' desire for dignity and identity, the merits of employee participation in decision making for certain categories of work, and the significant role of the corporate culture. This chapter also explores other major areas that seem to benefit from incorporating studies of social factors, and includes a discussion of policy implications, but not the theoretical paradigmatic issues involved.

Policy Implications of Allowing Shifting Preferences

Many neoclassical analyses take preferences as given and stable,[4] assuming that individuals have a particular and constant set of "tastes," "values," or "aspirations." Changes in behavior are assumed to result from changes in "constraints" or income, but not in preferences. Thus, for example, a neoclassical analyst investigating the reasons that the consumption of alcohol in the United States has declined since 1980 will typically ask if the price of alcohol has increased, whether the age of drinking has been raised, and so on, but not whether the desire to consume alcohol has been reduced because of changes in the valuation of "drinking." The neoclassical explanatory conceptions do not really accommodate the fact that these changes are due largely to two social movements: the health-and-fitness movement and the neotemperance movement, especially Mothers Against Drunk Driving, (MADD) and Students Against Drunk Driving, (SADD).

The reasons that neoclassicists treat preferences as fixed should be briefly explicated and arguments for disregarding these reasons provided. Information about preference changes, neoclassicists assert, is "ephemeral," based on "soft," nonbehavioral data such as surveys of attitudes; further, preference changes involve nonobservable states of mind. Without asking if or how such data can be used or made reliable, let us note that the *same* tools that are used to study economic factors can be used to study noneconomic variables, as they are reflected in actual behavior. For example, following Lancaster's approach,[5] one may disaggregate the attributes of a car to determine the price purchasers are willing to pay for each of the attributes, such as speed, design, and color. The *same* disaggregation can be used to determine the amount people are willing to pay for a car to be American or non-Japanese (say, after World War II) and the change (presumably the decline) in this preference over the postwar years. Other such values might include whether a car is "beautifully" designed, environmentally sound, and so on.

Neoclassicists argue that incorporating preference changes in the explanation of behavior precludes useful analysis, because whenever behavior changes, we presumably state that preferences have changed. There is, however, a satisfactory rebuttal for this argument. If we have several—or, preferably, numerous—observations over time, we can test hypotheses about changes in constraints *and* in preferences (including value changes that often cause preference changes). For instance, tax compliance has been shown to be affected both by the level of taxation (basically, the higher the tax rates, the lower the level of compliance) and by whether taxes are viewed as fairly imposed.[6] Thus, if an increase in compliance follows a period in which tax rates have not been reduced, and if in the same period numerous loopholes have been closed, all things being equal, we would expect that the change is due, in fact, to an enhanced perception of fairness.

The argument of some neoclassicists that they need not study preference changes or the value changes that drive them because these phenomena belong to "different" disciplines (namely psychology and sociology), may, indeed, be correct. It is an argument that favors the development of a more encompassing paradigm, one that encompasses both social and economic factors: socio-economics.

A key policy implication of a paradigm encompassing the study of changes both in constraints and in preferences is that when we design public policies, we need not limit our efforts to providing information (based on the assumption that people have fixed preferences but need to understand better the costs and benefits of the choices they face). Rather, we may also seek to appeal to people's values and affect new preferences by, for example, drawing on public education campaigns and on community leaders.

Several recent social movements catalyzed changes in the American public's values, changes that came about years or decades after relevant information was available. The civil rights movement of the 1960s brought both institutional reforms and a general change in the beliefs Americans held; blacks have come to be viewed more widely as full-fledged citizens, deserving social justice. The women's movement, which followed the blacks' push for civil rights, also achieved significant changes in America's values. Large segments of American society now consider the old adage, "A woman's place is in the home," not only outmoded but offensive. The recent shift in the attitude toward death further attests to changes in American values. Previously, a person was considered dead if his or her heart and breathing had stopped. Today, the idea of brain death has assumed primacy, largely because the health-care community adopted the standard. Other significant changes mainly occur when the social web of emotive forces found in peer groups supports behavioral change, such as in the recent condemnation of smoking.

Recently, the distinction between informing individuals and seeking ways to appeal to their values has been highlighted by the efforts to slow the spread of AIDS. In 1989 the Surgeon General sent a brochure to every home in the United States (and distributed pamphlets to drug addicts in the back alleys) informing Americans about the danger of AIDS and what is to be done. While this campaign demonstrates the government's concern and interest in changing Americans' behavior to stem the tide of AIDS, it is difficult to imagine a psychological process that would cause an addict to change his or her ways because of a piece of paper. Beyond this information campaign, finding means to involve addicts in support-ive social groups similar to Alcoholics Anonymous are needed (the nation's homosexuals, much more of a community than addicts, have been considerably more successful in changing their behavior).

In response to the argument for appealing to values in order to modify preferences, neoclassicists raise an ethical objection. They state that individuals ought to determine their own conduct (not the government), and that those who object to consumer sovereignty and seek to influence individual tastes are elitist snobs who wish to impose their "tastes" on others. Socio-economics takes a different normative stance, arguing that some "tastes" clearly ought to be modified—for instance, those that cause harm to others (e.g., smoking and reckless driving) and those that demonstrate open disregard for community needs (e.g., dumping toxic wastes into lakes). In other instances, it is proper to appeal to values people have, such as fairness.

Government is not the only instrument to influence tastes, nor is coercion the only proper means; the community is often the most effec-tive agent, and voluntary appeals are a main tool. Hence, community leadership and education by parents, neighbors, peers, and churches should be included in one's policy design. For example, smoking is being significantly curtailed as its social valuation is changing. Peer pressure plays a key role in generating the emotive force needed to help smokers mobilize themselves to overcome this addiction.

While socio-economists have identified many of the variables that affect preferences, there is no parsimonious conception of the factors that cause preference changes. Numerous factors are cited, but there is little consensus about the list. To illustrate in a very preliminary way the kind of propositions that are needed, it might be stated that social movements tend to have a set "natural history": they rise *rapidly* and then decay *gradually*, both through "secularization" (loss of commitment) and through sectarianism (internal divisions and strife). They rarely last. Hence, value changes based only on a social movement, if not followed by institutionalization, will have limited long-run effects and much smaller effects than is widely assumed at the height of the social movement.

If these propositions are correct, the long-term effects of a social-religious movement such as fundamentalist Islam, widely assumed to be a major factor in the Middle East in the coming decades, are likely to be quite limited. The same pattern is visible in the United States, where one can already witness the cresting and the beginning of the decline of the neotemperance movement, as well as perhaps even the health-and-fitness movement. The "couch potato" trend, a new movement of acquiescence that celebrates the comforts of home as an antidote to a perceived harshness in the economic environment, may be slowly ascending, only to follow the same pattern of other social movements: a rapid rise and a gradual decline.

It is not argued here that these propositions about the patterns of social movements have been sufficiently validated or are close enough to the data to be relied upon in policymaking. Rather, the propositions are used to illustrate the kind of parsimonious theory we need that would enhance the inclusion of the factors that shape preferences in socio-economic analyses and are used for policy analysis.

Education: Personality Development

Many educational reformers in the United States focus their agenda too narrowly by disregarding education, as distinguished from teaching skills, and transmitting knowledge or training. They leave out the need for basic psychological preparation, especially character formation, an essential prerequisite for acquiring basic skills and an essential in its own right to produce effective employees.

Plans to reform schools tend to overlook that about half of young Americans grow up in families that are not viable from an educational viewpoint. Frequent divorces, frequent rotation of boyfriends, and parents who come home exhausted both physically and mentally have left many homes with a tremendous parenting deficit. Instead of providing a stable home environment and the kind of close, loving supervision that character formation requires, many child-care facilities, grandparents, and babysitters mainly ensure that children will stay out of harm's way, but contribute little to their education.

As a result, personality traits essential for the acquisition of specific skills (math, "English," and vocational) often remain underdeveloped. Children come to school lacking self-discipline; they cannot concentrate, defer gratification, or mobilize attention to the tasks at hand. It is futile to pump into these youngsters more math, foreign languages, and long hours of science or liberal arts, as various commissions have favored.

Typing is a case in point. One can teach a person the mechanics in less than an hour (where to place the fingers, how to adjust the margins). The "rest" is a matter of patience, of self-discipline, to repeat the same drill long enough and often enough. Many studies have found that students cannot do math or write English. That is, they are not concerned with such advanced matters as whether students can craft a powerful essay or analyze a calculus problem; at issue is the ability to do arithmetic and write a clear memo. Again, close examination as to what is required points in the same direction. The elementary rules can be taught quickly. When you subtract A from B and get C, tally B and C to verify that they add up to A. A sentence ends with a period; it typically has a noun, and so on. The rest is a matter of self-discipline, the ability to adhere to these rules and not to jump to conclusions or ramble on in a paper.

One of the best bodies of data is that collected on a nationwide basis by James Coleman and his colleagues at the University of Chicago.[7] The data show that children who study well also have well-developed characters. Several other studies[8] reach similar conclusions. However, the strongest evidence is found in the success of programs such as the Conservation Corps and some of the drug-treatment programs. These take young people who are often disoriented and lacking in motivation and skills, and develop, first and foremost, their self-discipline, psychic stamina, and the ability to mobilize and make commitments. Once these are achieved, the acquisition of specific skills and employment becomes relatively easy.

Beyond being a prerequisite for good study habits, self-discipline is essential for making employees show up for work regularly and encouraging them to be responsible for the quality of their production, to take initiative, to observe work ethics.

What socio-economic policy would enhance the development of character? It is important to start early. Companies might offer their employees (mothers *and* fathers) more leave in the first two years of a child's development. Parents ought to be advised that a premature emphasis on cognitive achievements (learning to read, multiply, etc.) and neglect of human development is self-defeating. One presupposes the other.

Recognizing that such a transformation in child-care policy is unlikely, and that many parents will probably continue to spend relatively little time developing their child's character, public policy requires that schools step in. Schools may have to start earlier, say, at age four, and be open longer during the day and into the summer to make up for some of the lost parenting.

Finally, resources must be shifted from the top-heavy end of the educational structure to the lower levels: early education. Currently, we often prepare youngsters poorly in primary schools, mistrain them in high school, and then graduate them with poor work habits. All too often, then, we spend the first two years of college trying to correct what went wrong in the lower schools—teaching remedial English, catching up on math, and, above all, trying to instill better work habits. It is much more effective, from a sheerly economic viewpoint and a human one, to help young people learn things right the first time around.

Toward a Socio-Economics of Incentives

Policies are more concerned with "hierarchies" (such as within corporations and the government) than the market; markets are said to be best left on their own to build in self-regulating mechanisms. Here, the question of the most effective policies for compensating those subject to control and guidance by hierarchies is considered. Neoclassical analysis favors paying for performance rather than for time units (as is the case in paying wages or salaries versus paying by pieces of work acplished). The elementary reason is that when paying for time, one does not know what level of performance, if any, one pays for.[9] This is more than a mere theory; the widespread criticism of government and corporate bureaucracies is indicative of the problem.

The fact is, however, that pay for performance is rarely used.[10] Two studies illustrate the point. Medoff and Abraham[11] found that in two large corporations they studied, few financial rewards were offered for superior performance. In one corporation, employees whose work was ranked "not acceptable," the lowest rating, were paid only 7.8 percent less than the very best ("outstanding"). In another corporation, the difference between the pay of those whose work was "unacceptable" was only 6.2 percent less than that of those who topped six ranks, that is, the employees whose work was ranked "excellent." There was also a strong tendency to rank most employees as high performers. For example, in one corporation the performance of 95 percent of the employees was ranked "good" or better. Citing six different studies of the relationship between pay and performance, Lawler finds that

> evidence indicates that pay is not very closely related to performance in many organizations that claim to have merit increase salary systems . . . . The studies suggest that many business organizations do not do a very good job of tying pay to performance. This conclusion is rather surprising in light of many companies' very frequent claims that their pay systems are based on merit. It is surprising that pay does not seem to be related to performance at the managerial level.[12]

Socio-economics shows that the factor most important in explaining compensation is rank, not performance. While rank is indirectly linked to performance, bonuses would be more effective.[13] However, employees seeking relief from anxiety and wishing for power and visibility are more motivated by ranks, which helps to explain why ranks and not bonuses are by far the more common and important mode of differential compensation. The same factors account for the observation that when one tries to shift to greater reliance on pay for performance, the result is a very sharp drop in productivity, attendance, and other measures of performance. One group, composed primarily of psychologists and behaviorists, found that monetary rewards are counterproductive. For example, Deci "argues that money actually lowers employee motivation, by reducing the 'intrinsic rewards' that an employee receives from the job."[14] Slater similarly concludes that "using money as a motivator leads to a progressive degradation in the quality of everything produced."[15] Kohn

Kohn offers further explanation on the counterproductivity of monetary rewards: "First, rewards encourage people to focus narrowly on a task, to do it as quickly as possible, and to take few risks. . . . Second, extrinsic rewards can erode intrinsic interest. . . . [Finally], people come to see themselves as being controlled by a reward."[16]

Socio-economics does not conclude that competition policies cannot be modified to be somewhat more performance-oriented; however, a major shift may be neither possible nor beneficial because of the non-economic needs of the employees—including professionals and managers, not just blue collar workers. All of the studies cited here deal with these kinds of employees.

Institutional Change

Neoclassical analyses tend to focus on transactions among individuals or small units (such as households and small firms), and their aggregation in anonymous markets, that is, markets that are assumed to have no collective controls. To the extent that institutions are studied at all within this paradigm, they are generally perceived as reflecting arrangements made voluntarily and knowingly by individuals, in line with their interests and goals. Traditionally, other social sciences tended to view institutions as reflecting historical (macro) processes, societywide values, and power relations. Socio-economics seeks to encompass the influence of both individuals and society. It attempts to combine aggregative analysis with collective analysis by assuming that collective factors provide the context and are "priors" within which individuals act, and which in turn are affected by them.

The significance of systematically including institutional analyses lies in the fact that their existence hinders or assists policy, and hence, even if one does not seek to modify the institutions, their effects on policy must be taken into account. For example, a multiyear U.S. economic policy (say, a corporate development plan) that ignored the well-established economic effects of the four-year political cycle, driven by presidential elections, would be less likely to succeed than an economic policy that took the cycle into account. All other things being equal, the expansive policies of election years provide a much more hospitable economic environment for a new product, or newly expanded production capacities, than the first year of a new administration. "Bitter medicine" usually prescribed during this first year; hence, the period tends to be economically restrictive. The cycle, in turn, reflects the Constitution and not an aggregation of individual decisions. Similarly, one must expect little success for a policy that ignores differences among institutions (e.g., shifting law-enforcement functions from the FBI to local governments) because of the widespread corruption institutionalized in many local police forces. The same must be said about a policy that shifts responsibilities from the IRS or the Social Security Administration to local tax collection or welfare agencies.

Beyond accounting for the established features of existing institutions and the powerful inertial and vested interests they tend to generate, one must also recognize that institutions can be changed and policy advanced via such changes. Thus, instead of, or in addition to, using educational campaigns to encourage many millions of Americans to increase their saving, one can enhance saving by changing the tax laws by reducing, under some conditions, corporate outlays of dividends (i.e., by increasing retained earnings), or, more effectively, by reducing government expenditures.

Segregating Social Security from the unified budget and investing its surpluses into a portfolio of American corporate and government bonds would do as much or more for the American savings rate than would, say, doubling the size of funds individuals can salt away, tax deferred, into their IRAs. While a constitutional amendment to balance the budget may well create several new problems, it would modify significantly the institutional context of the struggle to reduce federal deficits.

Similarly, aside from working on individual incentive schemes, corporations often benefit when they introduce institutional changes such as increased cooperation with labor unions (e.g., General Motors and the United Auto Workers in recent years), quality circles, and participatory decision making. (None of these is automatically sure to have the desired result; more research is needed about the conditions that produce success.) One may argue whether individuals or institutions are more powerful; however, one conclusion is clear: policy analysis should consider both individual, aggregative factors and institutional factors.

Are Criminals Just Like Us?

Neoclassical economists analyze crime in terms of costs and benefits. They argue that the probability of being arrested and convicted, the size of the penalty, and the size of the loot (i.e., costs and "benefits") correlate with the frequency of a large variety of crimes being committed, including murder and rape.[17] The data are subject to considerable methodological controversies, but these need not concern us here. To the extent that these data have demonstrated that self-interest plays an important role in situations heretofore considered the domain of impulsive behavior, neoclassical economists provide an important correction to the overly socialized view of crime, a view that focuses almost exclusively on the role of education, subculture, peer pressure, and other such factors. However, to the extent that neoclassicists suggest that self-interest accounts for all or most of the variance, they vastly overstate their findings[18], and their conclusions will tend to mislead policymakers. Thus, for instance, Rubin's statements that "the decision to become a criminal is in principle no different from the decision to become a brick layer . . . the individual considers the net costs and benefits of each alternative and makes his decision on this basis," and that "tastes are constant and a change in [criminal] behavior can be explained by changes in prices [such as penalty]"[19] tend to mislead. They ignore the fact that despite whatever correlations are found between "prices" and level of criminality, much of the variance (in crime rates) remains unexplained, most likely because moral and other social factors are at work. Second, such statements overlook the fact that the "taste" for crime, like all others, is affected by normative and other social factors, such as the extent to which the relevant subculture disapproves of the particular kinds of crime involved.[20]

Similarly, statements such as Murray's that "crime occurs when the prospective benefits sufficiently outweigh the prospective costs"[21] are not only formulated in a way that makes falsification impossible (if no crime occurs under a given set of conditions under which it is expected to occur, the benefits might be said to not "sufficiently" outweigh the costs), but also tend to mislead policymakers into disregarding the role of education, subculture, leadership, and role models. Of special interest in this context is Wilson's discussion of the role of various "impulse control" movements and organizations in nineteenth-century America.[22]

Wilson points out that as industrialization advanced, youngsters who had once left their homes only to work under the watchful supervision of farmers or artisans, were starting to reside in boardinghouses in the cities, without any family bonds or authority. The result was widespread disorderly conduct. This rowdiness was met by numerous efforts to advance control of impulse and to build up inner control, self-discipline, and "character"; among them were Sunday schools, YMCAs, temperance movements, and various religious and secular voluntary associations. Some organizations had other goals, but impulse control was a welcome by-product; others were aimed directly at instilling self-discipline.

The policy point is that one needs to work not merely on the cost-benefit, deterrence, incentive, and police side, but also on the formation-of-preferences side, via moral education, peer culture, community values, and the mobilization of appropriate public opinion—factors that neoclassicists tend to ignore because they take preferences for granted, and their theories provide no analytical framework to conceptualize the ways in which preferences are formed and might be reformed. The trouble with theories that fit into a deontological paradigm is that they include numerous, complex propositions that are difficult to quantify. They may have to be synthesized, made more parsimonious and more operational, before they can effectively play their role next to economic analysis.

Neoclassical analysis of crime is largely based upon work pioneered by Becker, whose economic approach to white-collar crime is summarized by Posner: "The white-collar criminal . . . should be punished only by monetary penalties—by fines (where civil damages or penalties are inadequate or inappropriate) rather than by imprisonment or other 'afflictive' punishments (save as they may be necessary to coerce payment of the monetary penalty)."[23] Becker states that "according to the economic approach, criminals, like everyone else, respond to incentives."[24] By setting fines equal to the harm the corporate crime inflicts on society, companies will be deterred from certain crimes and society will be compensated for the harm imposed. Thus, Becker poses the question, "If guilty companies pay for the harm to society, why should we want to discourage white-collar crime that raises a country's wealth?"[25] Posner furthers this economic analysis of crime by arguing that fines can be an equally effective deterrent and are socially preferable because they are cheaper to administer than costly jail terms. He arrives at this conclusion using a cost-benefit analysis that weighs the cost of at this conclusion using a cost-benefit analysis that weighs the cost of collecting a fine against the cost of imprisonment. An important qualification is that the offender must be able to pay the fine, and that the fine be set equal to the disutility imposed by a jail sentence.

A socio-economic analysis of criminal sentencing is offered by Coffee, who argues that fines are an inefficient way to deter white-collar crime. He critiques Becker and Posner's optimal-sanctions approach (which he calls the Free Market Model), finding it flawed upon investigating "both traditional elements of economic analysis (such as uncertainty) and non-economic factors that are deeply embedded in the structure of our criminal justice system (such as the tendency toward nullification of extreme penalties)."[26] Whereas neoclassicists see fines as the optimal form of punishment, Coffee shows that the threat of incarceration is a greater deterrent than a monetary penalty.

Coffee also finds the Becker formula for determining an optimal fine too elusive to implement (there are too many unknowns left to be solved). He suggests we try to achieve equivalence between penalties, as opposed to determining precise monetary equivalents for a penalty. As, socio-economists explain, there are symbols involved in criminal sentencing as well as cut-and-dried costs. For example, Coffee criticizes Becker's model of punishment because it fines the rich and jails the poor. Values come into play as Coffee states that "criminal justice reforms must take into account the problem of demoralization costs." This represents an institutional bias, and "some means of seeking equivalence is necessary."[27] Answering this point, Posner retreats to his logic that there is a quantifiable fine equivalent for every prison sentence, and the offender should be imprisoned if the fine is not collected. He claims that Coffee's argument is "just a variant of the fallacy that imprisonment is inherently more punitive than fines."[28] He is left questioning how the rich are favored under such a system.

A Rand Corporation study is sensitive to the need for a dual perspective.[29] First, it deals with external costs of drinking alcohol and smoking cigarettes (costs not reflected in the price, such as making others sick), by itself a broader perspective than what many neoclassical studies use. Next, it uses the size of the excise taxes imposed, taxes that recoup some of the social costs not reflected in the pretax, market price. The study concludes that taxes on alcohol are not high enough, while according to economist Willard Manning who led the Rand team of researchers, those taxation"[30]—are high enough. (Costs are recouped, by the way, only because the study does not include the costs imposed on other members of the smoker's family—which would raise the external cost per pack, the authors says, from fifteen cents to thirty-eight cents—and because they deduct "contributions" smokers make to pension funds and Social Security [since they tend to die young, they often do not collect.])

Most important, the Rand study does not stop at evaluation from an economic efficiency viewpoint. It openly and explicitly calls attention to factors that might lead to the imposition of higher taxes on cigarettes than economic efficiency might call for. These are (1) signs that those who start smoking underevaluate the risk involved, higher taxes would act as a substitute for proper evaluation; (2) smokers show a desire to quit, and increased taxes would help accomplish their goal; (3) since smoking often starts at a young age (before one's preferences are formed) it is proper, as part of the societal reeducation effort, to use taxes to discourage formation of this preference, even if one holds that it is wrong to affect people's preferences once they have formed them.[31]

Conclusion

Using as a test criterion the ability to generate useful public policies, we examined an approach that encompasses both economic variables (of the kind neoclassical economists typically study) and other social, psychological, and political factors and found that this combination, called socio-economics, seems to yield more effective policies in several arenas. While it seems worthwhile to move toward the broader perspective afforded by socio-economics, it is also evident that additional work must be done to develop what has only been outlined here.

Notes

1. For additional discussion, see Amitai Etzioni, *The Moral Dimension: Toward a New Economics* (New York: The Free Press, 1988).
2. See, for example, Gordon F. Bloom and Herbert R. Northrup, *Economics of Labour Relations* (Homewood, IL: Richard D. Irwin, 1981); Lloyd G. Reynolds, Stanley H. Masters, and Coletta M. Moser, *Labor Economics and Labor Relations*, 9th ed. (Englewood Cliffs, NJ: Prentice-Hall, 1986).
3. Robert H. Frank, *Choosing the Right Pond: Human Behavior and the Quest for Status* (Oxford: Oxford University Press, 1985).
4. George J. Stigler and Gary S. Becker, "De Gustibus Non Est Disputandum," *American Economic Review* 67:76–90.

4. George J. Stigler and Gary S. Becker, "De Gustibus Non Est Disputandum," *American Economic Review* 67:76-90.
5. Kelvin Lancaster, "A New Approach to Consumer Theory," *Journal of Political Economy* 74:132-57.
6. Alan Lewis, *The Psychology of Taxation* (New York: St. Martin's Press, 1982).
7. James Coleman, Thomas Hoffer, and Sally Kilgore, Private and Public Schools (Chicago: National Opinion Research Center, 1981).
8. See, for example, Michael Rutter et al., *Fifteen Thousand Hours* (Cambridge, MA: Harvard University Press, 1979).
9. George P. Baker, Michael C. Jensen, and Kevin J. Murphy, "Compensation and Incentives: Practice vs. Theory," *Journal of Finance* 43 (July 1988):595.
10. Ibid.
11. Ibid., 607.
12. Edward E. Lawler III, *Pay and Organizational Effectiveness: A Psychological View* (New York: McGraw-Hill, 1971), 158.
13. Baker et al., "Compensation and Incentives," 601.
14. Ibid., 596.
15. Ibid.
16. Ibid.
17. See Ralph Andreano and John J. Siegfried, eds., *The Economics of Crime* (New York: Wiley, 1980); Simon Rottenberg, ed., *The Economics of Crime and Punishment* (Washington, DC: American Enterprise Institute, 1979).
18. Phillip J. Cook, "Punishment and Crime: A Critique of Current Findings Concerning the Preventive Effects of Punishment," in Economics of Crime, Andreano and Siegfried, eds., 127-36.
19. Paul H. Rubin, "The Economics of Crime," in Economics of Crime, Andreano and Siegfried, eds., 13-25.
20. Harold G. Grasmick and Donald E. Green, "Deterrence and the Morally Committed," *Sociological Quarterly* 22(1):1-14.
21. Charles A. Murray, *Losing Ground: American Social Policy 1950-1980* (New York: Basic Books, 1984).
22. James Q. Wilson, *Thinking About Crime* (New York: Vintage Books, 1985).
23. Richard Posner, "Optimal Sentences for White-Collar Criminals," *American Criminal Law Review* 17:409-18.
24. Gary Becker, "The Economic Approach to Fighting Crime," *Business Week*, June 10, 1985, 16.
25. Becker, "Tailoring Punishment to White-Collar Crime," *Business Week*, October 28, 1985, 20.
26. John C. Coffee, "Corporate Crime and Punishment: A Non-Chicago View of the Economics of Criminal Sanctions," *American Criminal Law Review* 17: 419-71.
27. Ibid.
28. Posner, "Optimal Sentences for White-Collar Criminals."
29. Willard G. Manning et al., "The Taxes of Sin: Do Smokers and Drinkers Pay Their Way?" *Journal of the American Medical Association* 261(11):1608.
30. Gene Koretz, "Economic Trends," *Business Week*, June 5, 1989, 27.
31. Manning et al., "Taxes of Sin," 1608-9.

8

Toward a Neo-Progressive Movement

How to Solve the Warming Effect

Scientists have come up with an ingenious solution to the problem of global warming. They propose to seed the oceans with 300,000 tons of iron, encouraging the growth of marine algae that would absorb excess carbon dioxide from the air by photosynthesis. A special panel of the National Research Council has endorsed the idea as valid and practical. "I think it is a good idea," stated Roger Revelle, former director of the Scripps Institution of Oceanography. "It is far more economically feasible than other options on the table," said Adam Heller, University of Texas at Austin. "You give me half a tanker full of iron," offered John Martin of the Moss Marine Laboratories, "I'll give you another ice age."[1]

Let us assume that preliminary tests prove that iron-seeding is satisfactory, and that additional evidence shows that the warming trend is heating up. We, as a community, thus face a threat we cannot deal with as individuals; moreover, we have a feasible technical solution. Yet, given the nature of our *political institutions*, we are likely to overheat anyhow or generate a new environmental threat.

Were Congress to consider ironing out the problem, the coast guard, navy, Environmental Protection Agency, and the National Oceanic and Atmospheric Administration would pepper the relevant congressional committees with repeated funding requests to support their iron-seeding projects. Their efforts would be underwritten by campaign contributions, junkets on the high seas, and honoraria for global-warming speeches by congressional "experts" from political action committees (PACs). Congressional members from iron-producing regions would demand that the iron be mined in *their* districts, contributing to an increase in the total amount of iron purchased. Furthermore, members from districts that produce zinc and copper would find studies that show that those metals, too, have salutary effects and insist that they also be cast into the ocean. Foreign lobbyists would insist, for the sake of continued negotiations on international trade concessions, that iron from Taiwan, Korea, Japan, and Brazil also be employed.

Ultimately, the amount of iron and other minerals cast into the seven seas (and, most likely, quite a few lakes for good measure) would vastly exceed what most scientists recommend. The result: further stress on an already strained budget, and possibly even the dawn of a new ice age.

From the TAA and EDA

Those who doubt that our political institutions are typically this compromised need only examine the numerous occasions in recent years when policies that were clearly designed to serve the national interest were rendered impotent or harmful after being run though our insidious political mill. Moreover, we shall see that despite the rather different circumstances in each instance, one systemic force consistently derailed good public policy.

Take, for example, the history of Trade Adjustment Assistance (TAA), passed in 1962 to help workers whose jobs had been eliminated by rising imports. Workers who could prove that government trade concessions were a major factor in their unemployment could receive supplementary benefits. From 1962 to 1974 only 35,000 workers qualified.[2] Then, Congress, under pressure from labor unions, select industries, and their lobbyists and PACs, introduced a new provision requiring only that workers demonstrate that imports were a "substantial cause" losing their jobs. Consequently, a program that cost the American taxpayers the relatively small sum of $9 million in 1973, cost $69.9 million by 1976, and $1.5 billion by 1980.[3] Moreover, by 1980 most of the aid was not going to workers in industries shrinking due to imports, but to workers who had been temporarily laid off.[4] Not surprisingly, when a recruiter from General Dynamics tried to convince laid-off steelworkers in Ohio to move to a plant in the Northeast, the workers were reluctant to do so: they didn't want to lose their substantial TAA benefits.[5] Thus, the program, after being warped by special-interest pressure, ultimately discouraged labor-force adjustment—the exact opposite of what was originally intended.

The story of the Economic Development Administration (EDA) is remarkably similar. Its original mission was to help areas of the country suffering significant economic stress by funding public works programs, technical assistance grants, business loans, and loan guarantees. In 1965, when the program began, 12 percent of Americans lived in areas that qualified as "distressed" and, hence, were entitled to special help.[6] By 1979 most of the U.S. population (84.5 percent) lived in areas that, because of congressional pressure, qualified as "distressed."[7] In 1982 EDA sought to decertify a number of obviously well-off areas, among them Beverly Hills. But Congress blocked the move, thereby destroying the possibility that EDA funds would be concentrated in areas with significant economic rehabilitation and development needs.[8]

In other instances, policy options are not even adopted because it is widely expected that, given our interest-driven political system, these policies will be readily perverted. For instance, several experts concluded that an industrial policy effectively developed for Japan by its Ministry of International Trade and Industry (MITI) ought *not* to be considered for the United States because the character of our political institutions is deficient. Both opponents and proponents of an American MITI, which would promote American competitiveness through strategic planning and public financing, worry that such a program would be victimized by our political system.

Economist George Eads, a former member of the White House Council of Economic Advisers and now a vice president of General Motors, testified before a congressional subcommittee about creating a national development bank—a vital tool of industrial policy. Although he agreed that it was needed, Eads opposed the bank, because he feared that it would turn into a political football.[9] Congressional members and special-interest groups, he predicted, would grab hold of the bank to funnel aid to their constituencies, disregarding the common goal of making the economy more competitive.

Beyond Allocation

While special-interest groups have been with us since the founding of the Republic and are commonplace in other democracies, their recent role in the United States has been especially venal. First, in our system, instead of limiting themselves to questions of allocation (dividing the pie), particular interests promote expanding the governmental pie, bloating federal programs so that everyone gets a piece of federal funding. For example, it would be less harmful if Pentagon experts ordered one antitank weapon system and Congress allotted the contract to defense contractor A (instead of B) because A was in the district of the Senate Armed Services Committee chair, or because it was the "turn" of congressional district Z to have A get the contract, and so on. At least we would get an antitank system that met expert specifications. More often, however, U.S. political institutions work to award the contract to districts X *and* Y *and* Z, ordering several antitank systems to make pork for more districts in order to be rewarded by still more industrial lobbies, labor unions, PACs, and others. This process is inflationary and leaves the government ineffectual because money is thrown at politically powerful projects while other needs go unattended.

The bailout of Social Security (helped along by a bipartisan commission) and the 1986 Tax Reform Act provide notable exceptions to the general rule that our legislative system is largely captured by special interests. But ordinarily—whether the government is dealing with issues such as gun control, textile import quotas, energy taxes, air bags, immigration policies, the "war" on drugs, or health-care costs—the nation cannot face a problem and expect that it will be met with a reasonable, workable public policy in the public interest. In the contemporary era of postmodern politics, public policy is twisted by the tribalistic behavior of our particular interests.

Public Misunderstanding

Democratic theory maintains that if "the people" are dissatisfied with the workings of a government, they are free to "throw the rascals out" and replace them with a new group, one that is more dedicated to their particular and community interests. The American public, however, is blind to systemic problems; hence, if the public does throw out one batch of representatives, the next batch will be about as beholden to particular interests as the previous one. For today, it is almost impossible to run for office in the United States and raise the enormous sums of money needed to run a viable campaign without becoming indebted to special-interest groups.

The public is not adequately aware of the situation because the media tend to highlight individual wrongdoing, recognizing that systemic flaws do not titillate people: as a culture, we tend to focus on psychological, individual explanations, not on structural, sociological ones. Generally, we consider it disloyal to find flaws in the system, and easier to criticize individuals. The public is thus not mobilized to favor systemic changes, and whatever reform zeal it may have dissipates after it replaces congressional members beholden to one set of special-interest groups with members indebted to another.

Pluralism without Unity

Some political scientists have argued that special-interest group representation *adds* to the democratic process. Communities have diverse needs and particular interests that must be satisfied to serve them; however, there are two kinds of pluralism: "unrestricted" and "encapsulated." In the case of the former, each group is out to gain all it can, with little concern for the community as a whole. In the latter, groups vie with one another, yet voluntarily limit themselves when they recognize common interests. American pluralism has been—and there is reason to believe it has increasingly become—mainly of the unrestricted kind, severely taxing the political institutions entrusted with crafting policies in the common interest.

The reasons are in part societal. Unlike other countries, the United States does not have many nationwide community-building institutions. We have a larger and less homogeneous society than most other democracies. Our highly fragmented educational system transmits many different values in thousands of distinct localities. Indeed, the very notion of a national curriculum, such as those followed in countries as diverse as France and Israel, is considered anathema, by most Americans, an extreme intervention by the federal government into local values and traditions. As a result, American youngsters grow up with relatively few shared values, symbols, and paradigms that many other communities draw upon to build consensus. We no longer have a national draft that draws people from various backgrounds together for years of service— the functional equivalent of the frontier. We have very few national newspapers. Public television is weak compared with the fragmented commercial networks, and local news coverage predominates, despite recent achievements by CNN and C-SPAN. Consequently, many social, economic, cultural, and political differences reach the national political institutions for processing without being accompanied by a community-wide consensus on which widely supported public policies might be built.

An ideology has developed, moreover, supported by some social scientists and intellectuals, which claims that there is no community-wide (or "public") interest, only the give-and-take of particular interests. Hence, it is argued, the actions of the interest groups are not detrimental; on the contrary, they are part of normal politics in which the "community" is served through service to its various constituencies.

I disagree with this position, first, because not all constituencies are served in this way. Only those needs that are represented by the politically powerful are met; vulnerable members of the community are neglected. Second, the long-term needs of the community and those shared needs that have no specific group payoffs are shortchanged. These needs include saving for future generations; national defense needs that yield no profits, such as salaries for the troops; and environmental protection.

I also reject the suggestion that one cannot tell common interests from particular interests. For example, when Common Cause fights to reduce the power of private money in public life, it is not seeking payoffs for its members; it is advancing what its members and leaders believe is in the common interest. This sort of cause is quite discernible from, say, an oil company's argument that it should be given a tax deduction because oil drilling is in the national interest. The criterion to be applied is this: Who benefits? If it is mainly the members of the group in question, then it is a particular interest, whatever the group's pronouncements dress it up to be. If the beneficiary is mainly the society at large, then a common interest has been found.

Still other political scientists have argued that one need not be concerned with special-interest groups because they neutralize one another. For instance, the Business Roundtable may favor a lower minimum wage, but labor unions endorse a higher one, leaving the legislature free to pursue the public interest. This model of interest-group representation could not be further from the truth: not all interest groups were created equal in economic and political power (compare, for example, the National Rifle Association to the gun-control lobby). Moreover, a well-heeled lobby is often pushing Congress from one side, while on the other side, the unorganized public at large is barely cognizant of what is happening. Notice, for instance, how lobbyists representing secondhand car dealers gutted reform legislation that would have required them to disclose known defects, even though such a law would have benefited the public.

Finally, it may be suggested that this line of argumentation is old hat. Political observers from David Truman to Theodore Lowi have chronicled the disruptive power of special-interest groups.[10] This does not mean that the message from these wilderness voices is any less relevant. What we need to concentrate on now is creating a consensus that special interests are at the core of our systemic problems. Such a conclusion would replace the facile "interpretations of the week," which locate the source of our political malaise in the president's timidity, the absence of term limitations, and other issues.

New Powers

It is not business as usual in the world of special-interest groups. While lobbying has always been with us and is constitutionally protected as a means for groups to articulate their special needs, the political power of special interests and the neglect of shared community needs has increased since the mid-1970s. Following the Federal Election Commission's 1975 advisory opinion on the legality of Sun Oil Company's SunPAC,[11] special-interest groups concluded that it was legal to provide large campaign contributions—contributions that obligate politicians to their big donors. Since then, the number of PACs has grown rapidly. There were 608 registered PACs in 1974;[12] by 1983 the number had more than quintupled to 3,371.[13] As of December 31, 1991, the number had grown to 4,094.[14] In 1974 PAC contributions made up 17 percent of the average campaign costs for candidates running for the House of Representatives;[15] by 1982 the percentage had risen to about 31 percent;[16] and by 1988, 37 percent of the campaign costs were being born by PACs.[17] Because these funds are much easier to obtain, compared with those raised from individuals, candidates favored by special-interest groups have a much better chance of being reelected than do those who are shunned.

Moreover, because special-interest groups tend to concentrate their money on incumbents (three-fourths of all PAC campaign contributions went to *re*election efforts)[18] on top of other factors that favor them, these candidates won more than 90 percent in recent congressional elections.[19] This money perverts the political process: politicians are not supposed to respond to the desires of the highest bidder; they are supposed to respond to the changing needs and interests of the community.

Secondary Corruption

The same political forces that caused this political maelstrom in the first place also disguise the problem, hindering attempts to correct it. Both of the major parties are deeply implicated; consequently, neither party is willing to confront the problem with serious reforms, even though a few Democrats and Republicans have made cursory efforts to stem the rising tide of PAC money. For example, what went wrong in the greatest raid in American history on the public till—the $500 billion S&L purse—was and still is largely hidden because both Democrats and Republicans receive hefty contributions and other favors from S&Ls.

Whatever the issue—whether it is the manufacture of $800 toilet seats for the Pentagon, the systematic supply of substandard parts for civilian aircraft, or the insidious practice of excessive physician referrals to medical labs owned by the referents—the public is often left in the dark because members of Congress are in bed with special-interest groups, which object to hearings, investigations, and legislation that would highlight issues that adversely affect their groups.

Finally, attempts to break the cycle of capital corruption by seriously limiting the flow of special-interest group monies and by legislating limits on campaign contributions are blocked by the very recipients of those monies: members of Congress.

A Question of New Political Energies

A Freudian diagnosis applies in this case to the body politic. There are no accidents; as a rule, when we observe a particular political symptom, there is an underlying cause. Thus, it is no accident that particular needs often take priority over the public interest. This pattern signals the powerful role that select groups within the society, (corporations, trade associations, labor unions, the National Rifle Association, the National Association of Realtors) take as they seek to extend their privileged position into the realm of politics. They overcome the egalitarian precept of one person, one vote, and replace it with a hegemony of special interests.

It further follows that if one seeks to counter these tendencies by striking a balance between particular interests and community interests, then merely good ideas, noble intentions, and well-crafted reform will not do. There must be a new source of political energy strong enough to propel the needed institutional changes, most especially, a sharp reduction in the level of private money in public life.

But where does the political muscle lie? We have here a prize political paradox. An imbalance exists because special-interest groups in toto are powerful, and they resist reforms because they don't want to lose their influence—perpetuating the cycle of capital corruption. Reformers, therefore, will have little luck if they try to change the system from within. Rather, give me a point of leverage outside the world, and I'll move the world, as Archimedes observed.

Where is the Archimedean point in our perverse polity? What is the source of the political energy needed to propel reforms? The ultimate protector of the common interest is the public at large. The power of special-interest groups is *not* based on their ability to serve most people via one interest group or another, but on the fact that most people, most of the time, are not politically active. This allows groups representing only small segments of society to distort national policies because their efforts go largely unopposed.

Some see the answer in mobilizing public opinion. Indeed, the media have been successful in alerting us to the dangers of excessive powers of particular interests; this force is insufficient, however. The public is preoccupied by many other issues and tends to mobilize more often on matters of substance than on process. Furthermore, the public's concern has been deflected by arguments that campaign contributions are a form of democracy. Most important, public opinion tends to be mercurial; it rises and falls as issue after issue sweeps through the political environment. The particular interest groups, by contrast, have staying power, occasionally yielding a bit to allow for limited reforms, but generally maintaining their chokehold on the Republic's policies.

Historical experience suggests that there is mainly one way to resolve the paradox: *Create a social movement.* As we know from the experience of the civil rights, women's, environmental, and neoconservative movements, social movements can succeed in redirecting the nation in significant, deep, and encompassing ways over decades. The reason social movements are much more effective than mere waves of public opinion is that they have a core of leaders (rather than being "led" by the media), strong shared values and molding symbols, and cadres that mobilize the rank and file to demonstrate, sit in, boycott, and take other steps needed to prod elected officials away from special-interest groups.

The Historical Model

The Progressive movement provides a direct precedent for the political cleanup and reform now needed, particularly since the movement grew out of an era that bears startling resemblances to our own. Progressivism arose in reaction to the enormous concentrations of wealth and political power that evolved in the United States following rapid industrialization during the late nineteenth and early twentieth centuries. The Industrial Revolution was created and carried forward by new American business plutocrats. Jay Gould, Andrew Carnegie, the Rockefellers, Harrimans, and Morgans amassed huge fortunes and monopolized business in many sectors by forming giant conglomerates or "trusts." They used their large concentrations of private power to direct public policy in a manner that reflected their interests in local, state, and federal governments. Those in the Senate—which was frequently called the "Millionaires Club," since so many senators were accused of having bought their seats—were frequently allied to narrow economic interests. Senators were often plied with favorable loans and offers of stocks at below-market rates. Immune to public anger, they consistently prevented tariff reform, election reform, and changes in the monetary system opposed by business.

As abuses became more prevalent and were brought to light by muckraking reporters and public investigations, more and more individuals dedicated themselves to becoming leaders and spokespersons for broad-based reforms. They and their expanding circle of followers were known as the Progressive movement. Unlike some of its predecessors, the new movement appealed to all classes, since its focus was on formulating proper rules of the game rather than serving particular interests. The movement, initially successful locally, elected Progressive mayors and governors, and later spread nationwide to support the elections of presidents Theodore Roosevelt and Woodrow Wilson.

Furthermore, the movement and its representatives supported many reforms that brought politics out into the open and curbed the intrusion of private power into the public realm. Local initiatives and referendums were introduced to allow more direct citizen participation in government. President Roosevelt enforced antitrust laws, prosecuting J. P. Morgan's Northern Securities railroad monopoly. He also pushed legislation through Congress to prohibit corporate contributions to candidates for federal office.

In 1913 a constitutional amendment was ratified providing for the direct popular election of senators, replacing their election by state legislatures that were deeply influenced by corporations. State legislatures, in effect, represented industries: "Ohio sent oilmen; Nevada sent silver mine owners; Maine, Michigan, and Oregon sent lumber barons; New York sent bankers. It was in a very real sense the ultimate pork barrel, a legislature of lobbyists," said one historian of the era.[20] President Wilson removed protective tariffs previously imposed at the urging of big business, and he established the Federal Reserve Board to regulate private banking in the common interest. While the details are numerous and complex, by seeking to reverse the intrusion of private power into public policy, the Progressive movement worked in two spheres. It limited the concentration of private economic power and reduced the influence of special-interest groups; it also pushed through political reforms that enhanced government responsiveness to the people. Historians differ in their regard for the Progressive movement. Some argue that it was too rationalist in its reliance on the civil service and "neutral" experts in public policies; others observe that the movement did not advance far enough. The latter point is almost certainly true and is but one more reason we now need another round of progressive reforms.

Toward a Neo-Progressive Movement

The public's current loss of control over political institutions calls for a new Progressive movement, a major social effort to energize a package of reforms that will reduce the role of particular interests in the Republic. As Robert Putnam and William Parent put it:

> At the close of this century, we are again faced with a haunting feeling that things have gone awry in our democratic institutions. The "splendid little war" in Iraq aside,

an array of problems frustrates elected representatives and policy makers operating traditionally out of the two-party system. . . .

It falls on all of us to ask ourselves what kind of government we want and to become participants toward that end . . . [21]

The details of the reforms and the specific reasons for favoring some over others are subjects that require an extensive, separate discussion. The following list illustrates the *kinds* of reforms that are needed:

1. A policy of financing congressional elections with public funds, such as we already have in place for presidential elections

2. Measures to curb the flow of money into politics (e.g., a ban on PACs, or a requirement that each donor designate the candidate to whom the contribution is intended, to avoid oligarchical pooling of money by PAC managers)

3. Efforts to reduce the costs of running for office (e.g., providing free media time and limiting the campaign period and the amount one may spend, as the United Kingdom does, to reduce the need for campaign contributions)

4. Measures that would promote the disclosure of the political process (e.g., creation of a lobby registry for all congressional and executive branch staff)

5. More effective enforcement of all rules, old and new, so reforms ought to include restoring the budgets and personnel of various watchdog bodies

True, several regulations that have been introduced in the recent past have failed to stem the flood of private money from special-interest groups into legislators' pockets and campaign chests. These regulations failed, however, because they were introduced in an erratic and piece-meal fashion; hence, the suggestion that the new reforms must be implemented as a package and may have to include more controversial measures as well, such as extending the term of House members from two to four years to reduce the need to campaign; prohibiting the use of federal funds for lobbying by recipients of government grants or contracts (e.g., defense contractors), and passage of a constitutional amendment that would allow Congress to write laws limiting private contributions to campaign funds and avoid technical objections previously raised by the Supreme Court.

Other lists might be drawn up to include measures that would help revitalize the political parties as counterweights to PACs and restore party discipline in Congress to reduce the number of "deals" with individual representatives. Even if all of the suggested reforms were implemented, additional measures might be needed. The main point, though, is that whatever reforms are called for, they will not be advanced until there is a significant new political vector; a public temporarily mobilized by the media will not do.

Common Cause is one of the few forces, together with Congress Watch, that is on the side of the public interest and champions many of the needed reforms. Common Cause, whose agenda is carefully honed around drafting and promoting reform legislation, must add to its approach the strategies of mass mobilization. Reforms will not be won merely by proposing legislation, offering amendments to reform bills, providing expert testimony, and other such measures. Steps must be taken that highlight the nefarious connections between legislatures and the interest groups that control them with campaign contributions: legislators need to be challenged constantly to explain their payoffs from special interests; call-in radio shows must be mobilized to oppose private money in public places as they were to check the raises Congress legislated for itself; and journalists must turn the public spotlight on special-interest lobbying.

The reforms must become the focus of a social movement whose leadership and cadres will keep millions of Americans focused on and committed to fighting for lasting major institutional reforms in local, state, and federal governments. Without a sustained effort, the reforms needed to bring public policy back under the control of genuinely democratic institutions will not take place. The public tends to be mobilized by muckraking for a while, only to return to its accustomed apathy. One must, therefore, use the periods of public outrage to introduce lasting institutional changes and to establish the countervailing factors that will curb special-interest groups even after the public zeal for reform is exhausted. Government by and for deep pockets must be replaced by a system that is based on the principle of one person, one vote.

Notes

1. William Booth, "Ironing Out 'Greenhouse Effect,'" *The Washington Post*, May 20, 1990, A1.

2. Michael R. Gordon, "Trade Adjustment Assistance Program May Be Too Big for Its Own Good," *National Journal*, May 10, 1980, 765.
3. Michael Reed, "The Administration Wants to Withdraw the Carrot of Trade Adjustment Assistance," National Journal, May 29, 1982, 958.
4. "That $1 Billion 'Surprise,'" *The Washington Post*, April 10, 1980.
5. Robert J. Samuelson, "On Mobility," *National Journal*, August 16, 1980, 1366.
6. Cristie Backley, Public Affairs Office of the Economic Development Administration, private communication, March 11, 1983.
7. Rochelle L. Stanfield, "EDA—The 'Perfect Vehicle' for Carter's Urban Strategy," *National Journal*, June 23, 1979, 1034.
8. Backley letter.
9. Statement of Professor George C. Eads before the Subcommittee on General Oversight and Renegotiation, Committee on Banking, Finance and Urban Affairs, U.S. House of Representatives, March 10, 1983, especially 6–7.
10. See David B. Truman, *The Governmental Process: Political Interests and Public Opinion* (New York: Knopf, 1951, 1964); Theodore Lowi, *The End of Liberalism* (New York: Norton, 1969).
11. *Dollar Politics*, 3d ed. (Washington, DC: Congressional Quarterly, 1982), 42.
12. Joseph E. Cantor, *Political Action Committees: Their Evolution and Growth and Their Implications for the Political System* (Washington, DC: Congressional Research Service, 1981, 1982), 56.
13. "Proliferating Political Action Committees," *National Journal*, January 29, 1983, 239.
14. "FEC Releases 1991 Year-End PAC Count," press release, Federal Election Commission, January 20, 1992.
15. Larry Makinson, *The Price of Admission* (Washington, DC: The Center for Responsive Politics, 1989), 15.
16. Ibid.
17. Ibid.
18. Larry Makinson, *The Price of Admission* (Washington, DC: The Center for Responsive Politics, 1991), 12.
19. Ibid., 13.
20. William Ashworth, *Under the Influence: Congress, Lobbies, and the American Pork-Barrel System* (New York: Hawthorn/Dutton, 1981), 107.
21. Robert D. Putnam and William B. Parent, "The Dawn of an Old Age?" *The Washington Post*, June 23, 1991, B5.

Index of Names

Aaron, Henry J., 52, 68fn, 69fn
Abraham, Katherine, 118
Alexander, Lamar, 25
Alperovitz, Gar, 30fn
Andreano, Ralph, 125fn
Ashworth, William, 140fn

Backley, Cristie, 140fn
Baker, George P., 125fn
Balcerowicz, Jan, 15
Barrett, Paul M., 49fn
Bayer, Ronald, 48fn, 69fn
Bayles, Michael D., 68fn
Beauchamp, Tom L., 68fn, 70fn
Becker, Gary S., 4, 49fn, 122, 123, 125fn
Bender, Mary, 97fn, 99fn
Berliner, Joseph, 10
Besinger, Peter, 49fn
Blahusiak, Jozef, 13
Blech, Benjamin, 73, 97fn
Blois, K.J., 19fn
Bloom, Gordon F., 124fn
Blume, Elaine, 86, 98fn
Bobinska, Lena Kolarska, 8
Booth, William, 139
Borgwardt, John, 109fn
Brimelow, Peter, 30fn
Bronson, Charles, 35
Brook, Robert, 58, 69fn, 70fn
Brownell, Kelly D., 76, 87, 97fn, 98fn, 99fn
Bruch, H., 88, 99fn
Bruin, Linda, 42
Burros, Marion, 97fn, 99fn

Califano, Joseph, 58, 72, 97fn
Callahan, Daniel, 57, 61, 62, 64, 68fn, 69fn, 70fn
Cantor, Joseph E., 140fn
Carnegie, Andrew, 136
Carson, Rachel, 106
Carty, James, 109fn
Childress, James F., 49fn
Clark, Mary, 49fn

Clinnard, Marshall B., 109fn
Coffee, John C., 123, 125fn
Coleman, James, 26, 30fn, 116, 125fn
Conner, Roger, 50fn
Cook, Phillip J., 125fn
Crenshaw, Theresa, 31, 48fn
Curran, William, 49fn

Daniels, Norman, 69fn
Deci, Edward, 118
Deutsch, Claudia H., 97fn
Duesenberry, James S., 20fn

Eads, George C., 129, 140fn
Engelberg, Stephen, 19fn
Etzioni, Amitai, 19fn, 20fn, 30fn, 50fn, 97fn, 99fn, 124fn
Evans, Glen, 49fn
Evans, Richard, 73, 97fn
Evans, Robert W., 69fn

Faux, Jeff, 30fn
Frank, Robert H., 124fn
Fuchs, Victor R., 52, 69fn, 70fn

Giuffra, Robert J., 109fn
Glassner, Barry, 36
Glastris, Paul, 49fn
Golenski, John D., 68fn
Goodin, Robert E., 49fn
Gordon, Michael R., 140fn
Gostin, Larry, 49fn
Gould, Jay, 136
Granzotto, Mark, 49fn, 50fn
Grasmick, Harold G., 125fn
Green, Donald E., 125fn
Griffin, Jean Latz, 50fn
Guerrero, Gene, 33, 48fn
Guthrie, Tanya, 97fn

Harper, Alfred E., 73, 97fn
Harrimans, 136
Heimbach, James, 84
Heller, Adam, 127

141

Subject Index

ACLU, 31-6: and AIDS, 34, 46-7; and authoritarian regimes, 33; drug testing, 33; and efficiency argument, 46; and radical individualists, 32; and sobriety checkpoints, 43; and X-ray machines, 31.
See also Constitutional Rights; First Amendment; Fourth Amendment
Administrative costs, and health care, 57
Aflatoxin, 78
AIDS: and the ACLU, 34, 46-7; and contact tracing and testing, 31, 34, 45; and health care, 59-60; and Helms, Jesse 47; and U.S. Surgeon General, 114.
See also HIV
Airline pilots, and drug testing, 38
Alaska, and Medicaid, 51
Alcohol, and neoclassical evaluation, 112
Alcoholics Anonymous, as a model support group, 114
Alexandria, Virginia, and drug trafficking, 43
Alzheimer's disease, 64
Ameliorative care, and health care, 64-5
American Heart Association, 89, 96
Amtrak, and drug testing, 39
Anorexia, 88
Anti-smoking legislation, and the slippery slope argument, 36
Arizona, and Medicaid, 51
Arms sales, and Syria, 13
Atco Properties & Management, and employee health benefits, 74

Balanced budget amendment, 120
Bill of Rights, 41, 44
Blue Cross & Blue Shield, 63
Bonding, between child and teacher, 28
Britain: and health care, 67; and health-care treatment allocation, 63; and kidney dialysis, 51
Business associations, 104-108

Business Roundtable: and ethics, 105, 107; and special-interest groups, 132

C-SPAN, 132
Campaign contributions, and health care, 57.
See also Special interests groups
Capital conversion, and post-communists countries, 10
Carbon dioxide, and global warming, 127
Catholicism; and ethic of acquiesce, 63; and the slippery slope argument, 36
Capitalism, shift from raw to mature in post-communist societies, 23
Center for Food Safety and Applied Nutrition, and dieting study, 88
Center for Science in the Public Interest, 96
Central planning, and health care, 57
Character formation: and Conservation Corps, 27, 116; and drug-treatment, 27; and family, 24-8
Chicago Tribune, 47
Child care, 25, 27, 31
Child labor, and the Age of Industrialism, 23
Children, 23-28; and education, 115-7
China, and democratization, 11
Christian Science Monitor, 4
Civic Groups, 93; and Common Cause, 132, 139; and Congress Watch, 139
Civil Rights Movement, and public values, 113
Clear and present danger, 37-40
CNN, 132
Colorado, and Medicaid, 51
Common Cause, 132, 139
See also Civic Groups; Special Interests
Communitarianism, 28: and voluntary associations, 96
Community, 28; and health maintenance 89-93; and special-interests groups, 132